Beyond Functional Assessment

Beyond Functional Assessment

A Social–Cognitive Approach to the Evaluation of Behavior Problems in Children and Youth

Joseph S. Kaplan

pro·ed
An International Publisher

8700 Shoal Creek Boulevard
Austin, Texas 78757-6897
800/897-3202   Fax 800/397-7633
Order online at http://www.proedinc.com

© 2000 by PRO-ED, Inc.
8700 Shoal Creek Boulevard
Austin, Texas 78757-6897
800/897-3202   Fax 800/397-7633
Order online at http://www.proedinc.com

Library of Congress Cataloging-in-Publication Data

Kaplan, Joseph S.
    Beyond functional assessment : a social–cognitive approach to the
evaluation of behavior problems in children and youth / Joseph S.
Kaplan.
        p.   cm.
    Includes bibliographical references.
    ISBN 0-89079-835-4 (pbk. : alk. paper)
    1. Behavioral assessment of children.   2. Behavior disorders in
children.   3. Problem children—Education.   I. Title.
LB1124.K26   2000
371.93—dc21   99-41749
                                                      CIP

Production Director: Alan Grimes
Production Coordinator: Dolly Fisk Jackson
Managing Editor: Chris Olson
Art Director: Thomas Barkley
Designer: Jason Crosier
Print Buyer: Alicia Woods
Preproduction Coordinator: Chris Anne Worsham
Assistant Managing Editor: Martin Wilson
Project Editor: Sue Carter
Publishing Assistant: Jason Morris

Printed in the United States of America

2   3   4   5   6   7   8   9   10   04   03   02   01

Contents

Introduction

The Task Analytical Model

Several years ago, my colleagues and I wrote a book called *Evaluating Exceptional Children: A Task Analysis Approach* (Howell, Kaplan, & O'Connell, 1979). As the title implies, the major topic of that book is an educational evaluation process we referred to as "the task analytical model." The underlying premise of this model is that if a student does not engage in behavior deemed desirable by the school, he or she probably lacks one or more of the prerequisites necessary to engage in that behavior. This premise did not originate with us. We borrowed heavily from the work of Robert Gagne, who wrote, "A student is ready to learn something new when he has mastered the prerequisites; that is, when he has acquired the necessary capabilities through preceding learning" (1970, p. 27). For example, if we apply Gagne's premise to a student having difficulty computing simple addition facts, we might hypothesize that the reason for his difficulty is that he has not mastered all of the prerequisites for the task (e.g., reading numbers, writing numbers, reading and understanding operation signs, etc.). By listing *and assessing* all of these prerequisites, we can determine which ones the student lacks. This tells us why the student is having difficulty with the task and what needs to be done to remediate the problem.

In a follow-up text, *Diagnosing Basic Skills* (Howell & Kaplan, 1980), we extended the application of the task analytical model to interpersonal (i.e., social) behaviors. For example, if a student has difficulty interacting with peers without being aggressive, we might hypothesize that the reason for her difficulty is that she has not mastered all of the prerequisites for the "task" of being assertive (e.g., understanding the rule about fighting at school, being aware of when she is being aggressive and when she is being assertive, being able to control her emotions to the extent that she can stop herself from being aggressive, knowing how to interact with peers assertively, etc.). Just

as we did in the academic (arithmetic) problem, we try to determine which, if any, of these prerequisites the student lacks. Once we know this, we know why she has difficulty interacting without aggression and what needs to be done to remediate the problem.

Beyond Functional Assessment

I first introduced the task analytical model to graduate students in special education at Portland State University 2 decades ago. Since then, hundreds of teachers in training have been exposed to the model and while some have used it in their own classrooms, the majority of them have not. Why? Feedback, from both beginning and veteran teachers, suggests that although they like the simplicity of the model and the structure it provides, they dislike having to generate all of the prerequisites, assessments, and objectives for all of the student behaviors they need to assess. If someone else did the work and provided them with all of these materials in one complete, easy-to-use package, they would use it. It has taken a long time, but I believe that *Beyond Functional Assessment* (Beyond FA; pronounced Beyond Fahhh!) is that package. It provides all of the prerequisites, assessments, and objectives a teacher needs to evaluate 10 of the most troublesome student behaviors.

What Beyond FA Does

First, and foremost, Beyond FA can be used to evaluate the causes of student behavior problems. It provides information about why a student is misbehaving and what you can do about it. This evaluation can occur at any juncture in a student's school life. For example, if a student is having behavior problems in a general education setting, a member of a Teacher Assistance Team can use Beyond FA as part of a prereferral process to determine the cause of the problem and design an intervention to be implemented in the general education setting. If the intervention works, the student stays where he is. If it doesn't work, he can be referred for a more comprehensive evaluation to determine whether or not he is eligible for special education services.

For the student already placed in a special education program, Beyond FA can provide the teacher with information used to design an intervention for implementation in the special education setting. It also provides special educators with performance objectives for social behaviors that can be included in the student's Individualized Education Program (IEP).

Beyond FA can be especially useful to educators working with students with emotional or behavioral disorders (EBD). A large part of the curriculum in an EBD classroom involves instruction in social skills—those discrete interpersonal behaviors such as being assertive, sharing, and giving and receiving compliments. Unfortunately, the research on social skills training is not very encouraging (Mathur & Rutherford, 1996). Apparently, students learn the skills but tend not to use them. Advocates of social skills training suggest that students who don't use these skills either have a skill deficit (i.e., they *don't know how* to use the skill) or a performance deficit (i.e., they *don't want* to use it). They are either not able or not willing. This seems an oversimplification of the problem. Knowing how and wanting to are not the only prerequisites students need to use a social skill. There are at least four or five other personal prerequisites, not to mention environmental prerequisites. Beyond FA includes all of these prerequisites (and their assessments) and can be used to determine why students don't use the social skills they are taught.

In other EBD settings, the term *social skills training* is used as a rubric for a curriculum including any number of cognitive and cognitive-behavioral self-help programs such as (but not limited to) self-management, self-instructional training, verbal mediation, problem solving, cognitive restructuring, and stress and anger management. No one student in an EBD classroom needs *all* of these programs. A few might need anger management, while others might be better off learning problem solving. Still others might benefit the most from cognitive restructuring. The teacher in this setting has two options: (a) pick one program such as social skills training or problem solving and teach it to all of his or her students, even though some of them might profit more from one of the other strategies; or (b) individualize his or her social skills curriculum by using Beyond FA to assess the needs of individual students and give *each one* the program he or she needs the most.

Although it may seem easier to choose one strategy (eeny-meeny-miny-moe) to teach to all students, this approach really isn't cost-effective over time. As with most important things in life, you can either pay now (in terms of effort) or pay later (in terms of failure).

And last, but certainly not least, Beyond FA lives up to its name by helping school districts meet the new discipline requirements set forth in the Individuals with Disabilities Education Act Amendments of 1997 (IDEA Amendments). This legislation mandates that school districts contemplating severe disciplinary action (e.g., long-term suspension or expulsion) against a student with a disability first implement a behavioral intervention plan (BIP) based on a "functional behavioral assessment" (FBA) of that student's behavior (p. 98). To understand how (and why) Beyond FA can help educators meet this requirement, we must first examine the theoretical models upon which FBA and Beyond FA are based.

The original FBA was developed years ago by behaviorists working in settings for individuals with severe disabilities. Because many of these individuals lacked the expressive language needed to verbalize their wants, they often communicated them through behavior other than speech. Although such behavior was considered undesirable, it was often inadvertently reinforced by someone in the environment. Individuals who wanted attention hurt themselves and were attended to. Those who wanted to be left alone screamed and were left alone. Figure 1.1 illustrates this model of learning.

Once behaviorists figured out that they were actually strengthening behaviors they wanted to weaken (and weakening behaviors they wanted to strengthen), they began collecting and analyzing data on behavior and on environmental events (e.g., antecedents and consequences) to better understand the function of the behaviors they wanted to change. This process of collecting and analyzing data is what the IDEA Amendments apparently

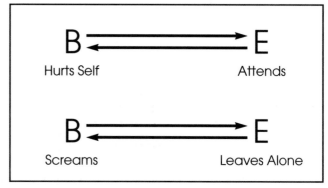

Figure 1.1. Learning based on behavioral (operant) model.

means by a "functional behavioral assessment." And, although the FBA is a marked improvement over the use of normative personality and projective measures in evaluating the cause of student behavior problems, it tends to be limited by its overreliance on the environment.

As someone trained in behaviorism, I fully understand and appreciate the role the environment (both physical and psychosocial) plays in shaping and maintaining much of our behavior. Still, I have difficulty accepting the idea that environmental events *alone* shape and maintain *all* human behavior. I prefer the social-cognitive view of Albert Bandura and his theory of reciprocal determinism (Bandura, 1974, 1977, 1986): Human behavior is the result of reciprocal influences between the personal variables (internal) of the individual, the environment (external) in which the behavior occurs, and the behavior itself. Figure 1.2 is a diagram of reciprocal determinism showing the most common personal (P) and environmen-

tal (E) variables that influence behavior (B). The same environmental event (i.e., antecedent or consequence) can be experienced differently by several different people. How this event shapes and maintains their behavior depends, to a great extent, on the personal variables of each individual. The traditional FBA does not take these personal variables into account. Therefore, when used alone, the FBA may not always provide all of the information needed to help change student behavior. This could have serious consequences for students with disabilities facing suspension or expulsion from school. My recommendation is to start with an FBA and, if not satisfied with the results, *before giving up on the student*, try Beyond FA. We owe it to our students to do a little extra if that's what it takes to keep them in school. For more information regarding the FBA, see Fad, Patton, and Polloway (1998); O'Neill, Horner, Albin, Storey, and Sprague (1990); and Sugai and Colvin (1989).

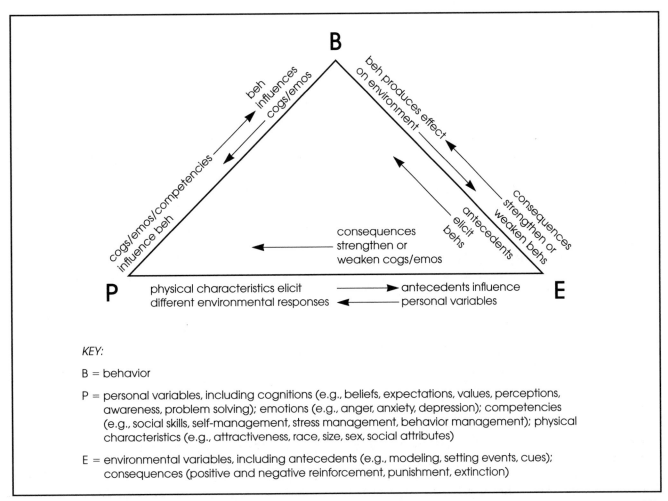

Figure 1.2. Reciprocal determinism applied to behavior problems. From *Beyond Behavior Modification* (3rd ed., p. 13), by Joseph S. Kaplan with Jane Carter, 1995, Austin, TX: PRO-ED. Copyright 1995 by PRO-ED. Reprinted with permission.

How Beyond FA Works

In FBA, we attempt to discover the purpose or function of the maladaptive behavior. We then teach the replacement target behavior that will achieve the same function. We support the new behavior by changing environmental variables. This is sometimes enough. But sometimes the replacement behavior doesn't "take." This may be because the behavior does not achieve the same outcomes (e.g., attention, escape), because it does so less efficiently, or because the environment doesn't support the new behavior. But it also may be that the student does not learn/use the replacement behavior because he or she lacks the prerequisites.

There are four basic steps in Beyond FA:

1. Identify the maladaptive and target behaviors.

2. List all of the prerequisites needed to engage in the target behavior.

3. Evaluate the current status of each prerequisite.

4. Interpret the results of the evaluation.

Let's examine each of these steps in detail.

Maladaptive and Target Behaviors

The first step in Beyond FA is to identify the maladaptive and target behaviors. The maladaptive behavior may be thought of as "any behavior that interferes with the physical, emotional, social, or academic well-being of the target student or any other person (affected by his or her behavior)" (Kaplan, 1995, pp. 59–60). The maladaptive behavior is what the student does now.

The *target behavior* (i.e., replacement behavior and functionally equivalent behavior) is the behavior exhibited by the student at the successful conclusion of an intervention. It is what you want the student to do. Ideally, the target behavior should be a fair-pair behavior and should achieve the same function as the maladaptive behavior. A *fair-pair behavior* is one that, when strengthened, results in the weakening of the maladaptive behavior. To be a fair pair, a target behavior must also be in the student's best interest. For example, "hits *self* when angry" is a target behavior for hits *peers* when a young man is angry, but it is not a fair pair. True, you can weaken "hits others" by strengthening "hits self," but it is not in the student's best interest to have him punch himself in lieu of punching others. An acceptable fair pair for "hits peers when angry"

is "tells peers how he feels when angry." The more times the student communicates his feelings with his words, the fewer times he is likely to do so with his fists. Also, telling others when he is angry is in his best interest because talking with others enhances his social and emotional well-being, not to mention his physical health (by avoiding fights).

Although Beyond FA does not cover *all* of the maladaptive behaviors students engage in at school, it does include those behaviors that many general and special educators consider objectionable. The 10 maladaptive behaviors in Beyond FA are described below in order of concern to teachers from least to most objectionable; many are behaviors that are likely to result in serious disciplinary action, such as long-term suspension, expulsion, or interim alternative education placement. The maladaptive behavior is listed first along with the letter code for the behavior inside (in parentheses). The maladaptive behavior is then described. The fair-pair target behavior is listed last. If your student or students engage in more than one of the behaviors described below, I recommend that you begin working with the one behavior that might respond most readily to treatment instead of tackling all of them at once.

1. *Does not work on assigned tasks unless closely supervised* (WKS/SUP): This student does not work on assigned tasks unless an adult is standing over him providing verbal encouragement or the threat of punishment. Although he is frequently off task, this student is not necessarily disruptive. Target: *Works on assigned tasks with minimal or no supervision.*

2. *Engages in physical activity inappropriate according to frequency, situation, and setting* (INAPP/MOVE): This student is frequently "on the move." She constantly gets in and out of her seat and often runs in the classroom and in the halls. This behavior could include movement considered stimulating to the student, such as rocking in place, but only if the movement disrupts the learning process in the classroom. Target: *Engages in physical activity that is appropriate according to frequency, situation, and setting.*

3. *Does not follow (or is slow to follow) directives expected of all students* (NONCOMP): This student does not comply with directives given by the teacher unless they are repeated several times, and sometimes he does not comply at all. Other times he may "comply" but in a way that is unacceptable to the person making the request. For example, when asked to hand in his work by putting it in a tray on the teacher's desk, he might do this as quickly as his peers, but the papers are tossed in the tray so that parts of the assignment are in the tray, on the teacher's desk, or on the floor. He often enters into a power struggle with adults over a compliance issue. This student is generally

noncompliant regardless of what he is told to do or who tells him to do it. Target: *Follows directives expected of all students, the first time given.*

4. *Engages in disruptive behavior when seeking attention from peers or adults* (DIS/ATT SEEK): This student interrupts the teacher from teaching and/or her peers from learning by making inappropriate noises, talking loudly, calling out, and/or engaging in excessive movement (e.g., jumping up from her seat). Target: *Seeks attention from others in nondisruptive manner.*

5. *Engages in tantrum behavior when requests are not met* (TANT/REFUS): This student cries, screams, curses, destroys, or throws objects when his demands are not met by peers or school faculty or staff. Target: *Engages in socially appropriate behavior when requests are refused.*

6. *Makes demands of others and threatens negative consequences if compliance is slow or demand is not met* (EXTORT): This student makes demands of others rather than requests. If others don't immediately accede to her wishes, she threatens them with physical harm (e.g., "You better if you know what's good for you!"). Other forms of intimidation are more subtle, such as facial expressions (glaring), gestures, or proximity (getting too close). Target: *Makes requests of others and, if request is refused, repeats request or accepts refusal.*

7. *Handles property of others in destructive manner* (DEST PROP): This student displays a total disregard for the rights of others by abusing their property. He grabs work, papers, pencils, crayons, and the like from others and tears, crumples, and breaks them, usually in full view of the victim. He may also engage in acts of vandalism of school property by writing on or scratching furniture or walls. This is not necessarily a student who is acting out of rage or frustration. Target: *Handles property of others in nondestructive manner.*

8. *Engages in aggressive behavior when provoked* (AGG/PROV): This student tends to be overly sensitive to criticism or baiting from peers. She may have a poor self-image and/or be short tempered with little or no anger or impulse control. She typically responds to peer provocations by hitting, kicking, shoving, or throwing objects, all with an obvious intent to harm the provocateur. She also responds with profanity, threats, and/or otherwise abusive language, which conveys her upset feelings over the provocation. Target: *Engages in assertive behavior when provoked.*

9. *Engages in verbally aggressive behavior without provocation* (VERB AGG/NO PROV): This student uses language in an abusive way toward others without any obvious provocation on their part. He threatens them, curses at them, baits and teases them, insults them, and voices his disapproval of them whenever he can. Target: *Interacts with others without verbal aggression.*

10. *Engages in physically aggressive behavior without provocation* (PHYS AGG/NO PROV): This student may be the class or school bully. She may be the acting-out, overtly aggressive student also known as "conduct disordered." She hits, kicks, and shoves peers, and throws objects at them with an obvious intent to harm—all without any overt provocation on their part. This behavior is often used as a form of intimidation and coercion. Target: *Interacts with others without physical aggression.*

Prerequisites

Personal Prerequisites

After identifying the maladaptive behavior you want to work on, you need to list all of the prerequisites the student needs to engage in the fair-pair target behavior. A student needs six generic prerequisites in order to engage in the fair-pair target behaviors listed above. These prerequisites are explained below. The prerequisite appears first, followed by a one- or two-word descriptor in parentheses, and then the description.

1. *The student understands the behavior expected of him (expectation):* In other words, the student understands the rule(s) he is expected to follow. I use the term *understand* instead of *know* because it is possible for someone to have knowledge of a rule but not comprehend it. We often think our students understand what behavior is expected of them and, in fact, it could probably be argued that of the six generic prerequisites listed, most students are likely to have this one. There are, however, some situations where this might not be the case. For example, students with deficits in receptive language and/or low cognitive ability may not understand all of the rules regarding classroom conduct, especially if they have not been carefully explained. Rules may be different at home than at school; culture plays a big part here. Some teachers may be inconsistent in enforcing their rules, or they may consistently enforce different rules for different students. Other teachers may be vague (sometimes deliberately so) in cueing their students to follow certain rules. Don't assume that all students know what the teacher means when he says, "Stop 'fooling around' and get to work!" Don't assume that all students define *fighting* the same way the teacher does.

2. *The student is aware of her behavior (self-awareness):* Suppose you want a student who often uses profanity to stop swearing and use more socially acceptable language; or you want a student who is frequently off task to complete her assignments in the time allowed. In each case,

the student has to be aware of her behavior before we can expect her to change it. Sometimes people become so habituated to (i.e., used to) their own behavior that they are not aware of it even as it occurs. If the student doesn't know when she is behaving appropriately or inappropriately *at the time she is behaving,* how can we expect her to stop it and do something else?

3. *The student is able to control his behavior (self-control):* Many biophysical and emotional variables can influence a student's behavior. What often seems like "willful disobedience" may actually be the result of something the student currently has little or no control over. Table 1.1 lists a number of maladaptive behaviors (includ-

ing those covered in this program), along with those biophysical and emotional factors that may contribute to the behaviors. These can also be temporary or occasional setting events such as lack of sleep, hunger, or stress caused by conflicts with others (e.g., a fight with Mom before school).

4. *The student knows how to engage in the target behavior (competence):* In order for students to complete all of their assignments independently (without cheating or copying) and turn them in on time, they must have all of the academic skills and knowledge necessary to complete the work on their own. If you want your students to behave assertively in response to peer teasing, they must

Table 1.1
Self-Control Factors and Maladaptive Behaviors

Emotional Factors

1.0 *Anger* may influence self-control in the following maladaptive behaviors:

  1.1 verbal and/or physical aggression (with or without provocation)
  1.2 noncompliance
  1.3 destruction of property of others
  1.4 tantrum when requests refused
  1.5 physical or verbal intimidation of others to get own way

2.0 *Anxiety* may influence self-control in the following maladaptive behaviors:

  2.1 passivity in face of aggression, manipulation, and/or criticism (from adults or peers)
  2.2 social isolation (student is withdrawn and doesn't speak to others unless spoken to)
  2.3 excessive and inappropriate movement (e.g., out of seat, running in classroom or halls)
  2.4 noncompliance (performance anxiety)
  2.5 disruptive attention seeking

3.0 *Depression* may influence self-control in the following maladaptive behaviors:

  3.1 social isolation
  3.2 off task (works only with close supervision)
  3.3 truancy
  3.4 noncompliance

Biophysical Factors

4.0 *Temperament Traits* may influence self-control in the following maladaptive behaviors:

  4.1 noncompliance (low approach–high withdrawal)
  4.2 off task (works only with close supervision; high distractibility; low attention span and low persistence)
  4.3 aggressive or other inappropriate responses to criticism or peer provocation (low threshold and high intensity of response)

5.0 *Impulsivity* may influence self-control in the following maladaptive behaviors:

  5.1 excessive and inappropriate movement
  5.2 disruptive attention seeking
  5.3 destruction of others' property
  5.4 verbal and/or physical aggression (with or without provocation)

6.0 *Sensory Impairment* (e.g., hearing or vision loss) may influence self-control in the following maladaptive behaviors:

  6.1 off task (works only with close supervision)
  6.2 noncompliance

(continues)

Table 1.1 *Continued.*

7.0 *Allergic Reaction* (or reaction to medications) may influence self-control in the following maladaptive behaviors:

   7.1 off task (works only with close supervision)
   7.2 noncompliance
   7.3 verbal and/or physical aggression (typically with provocation)
   7.4 excessive and inappropriate movement

8.0 *Neurological Dysfunctioning* (e.g., attention-deficit/hyperactivity disorder (ADHD), Tourette's syndrome, petit mal seizures) may influence self-control in the following maladaptive behaviors:

   8.1 off task (due to distractibility associated with ADHD; seizure activity, e.g., petit mal)
   8.2 excessive and inappropriate movement (due to hyperactivity associated with ADHD)
   8.3 disruptive attention seeking (due to impulsivity associated with ADHD)

9.0 *Metabolic Dysfunction* (e.g., hypo- or hyperglycemia, diabetes) may influence self-control in the following maladaptive behaviors:

   9.1 excessive inappropriate movement
   9.2 disruptive attention seeking
   9.3 any aggressive behavior (e.g., verbal, physical, destructive) accompanied by irritability and mood swings

Other Factors

10.0 *Communication Disorder* (speech and/or language impairment) may influence self-control in the following maladaptive behaviors:

   10.1 noncompliance
   10.2 off task (unless closely supervised)
   10.3 aggressive behavior (associated with frustration)
   10.4 social isolation

11.0 *Diversity* (e.g., language barrier, social mores, learning styles) may influence self-control in the following maladaptive behaviors:

   11.1 noncompliance
   11.2 disruptive attention seeking
   11.3 excessive inappropriate movement
   11.4 "cheating" (i.e., sharing work with others)
   11.5 off task (unless closely supervised)
   11.6 social isolation
   11.7 aggressive behavior (with provocation)
   11.8 passivity in face of aggression, manipulation, and/or criticism (from adults or peers)

know what to say, as well as how and when to say it. In short, we cannot assume that all students know how to "behave" the way we want them to.

5. *The student considers the consequences of engaging in the target behavior more rewarding (or less aversive) than the consequences of engaging in the maladaptive behavior (motivation):* It is not enough for the student to be able to predict what happens when she engages in the target behavior; nor is it enough for her to like the consequences of the target behavior. In order for the student to consistently and successfully engage in the target behavior, she has to like the consequences of the target behavior *more than* the consequences of the maladaptive behavior. For example, a student may know that when she stays on task she earns points that she may trade in for valued backup reinforcers

at the end of the school day. She may also like the social praise she gets from the teacher when the points are awarded. However, she may also like to talk to her peers. In fact, she may value talking to her peers more than she values acquiring points or receiving teacher praise. Positive peer attention is a powerful reinforcer, especially for pre-adolescents and adolescents. In this situation, the teacher must try to identify a more powerful reinforcer than talking to peers or come up with a more powerful aversive such as losing points already earned. Whatever decision the teacher makes, the student must consider the consequence(s) of being on task more rewarding than talking to her peers.

6. *The student does not hold any beliefs that are incompatible with the target behavior (beliefs):* This prerequisite is

not necessarily *essential* for the student to engage in the target behavior on an extrinsic level. A student may not enjoy doing his assignments and may hold some negative beliefs about school and still attend school and get his work done as long as he receives some powerful incentives from the environment (e.g., tokens and backup reinforcers). However, if you want the student to eventually internalize the target behavior so that it will generalize across settings and maintain over time, it is necessary that he only endorse beliefs that are compatible with it. For example, if you want the student to complete his work assignments and/or persist in the face of adversity instead of giving up, he must believe that there is a direct relationship between what he does and what happens to him. If, instead, he believes that what happens to him is controlled by fate or chance or a teacher who doesn't like him, he may simply consider himself unlucky and give up.

The degree to which an individual believes that he is able to influence the outcomes of situations is referred to by social cognitivists as *locus of control* (Rotter, 1966). Students who believe they have little or no influence over the outcome of situations in their lives are called "externals." They tend to believe that if something good happens to them they were lucky, and if something bad happens it's the teacher's or a peer's fault (e.g., "I don't do too good in her class because she doesn't like me."). Students with an external locus of control may not only fail to internalize target behaviors, but they may also not even engage in appropriate behavior at the extrinsic level because they are convinced that they have little control over the rewards and punishment they receive.

Locus of control is not the only belief that can influence the student's behavior. *Self-efficacy* (Bandura, 1977) refers to students' expectations (i.e., beliefs) about whether or not they can engage in a target behavior ("Can I do it?") and whether or not the target behavior will be effective in getting them what they want ("Will it work?"). For example, a student who responds aggressively to peer teasing may believe that she can't respond assertively and/or that assertive responding won't result in the cessation of the teasing. This lack of self-efficacy makes it difficult for the student to engage in the target behavior.

Students who believe that "it's terrible if things don't go my way" may never learn to accept criticism. Others who believe that "schoolwork is dumb" may continue to be truant, tardy, come to class unprepared, and/or not do their work. The student who believes that "it's terrible when I fail" may not do his work, either. The student who believes that "it's terrible if everybody doesn't like me" may continue to be the class clown and find it difficult to refrain from calling out or making faces during a group discussion. The student who believes that "if people do

things to me that I don't like, they are bad people and must be punished" will have a hard time interacting with his peers without behaving aggressively toward them. Likewise, the student who believes that "it's not macho to walk away from a fight" will have trouble staying out of fights. All of these students will have difficulty engaging in the target behavior because they endorse a belief that is incompatible with that behavior.

Please note that Beyond FA has included all of the above prerequisites for each of the 10 maladaptive behaviors covered in the program. These prerequisites are written specifically for a given maladaptive and target behavior and may be found in the first column on the Beyond FA worksheets under the heading "Prerequisites" (see Section 3).

Unique Prerequisites

In addition to the aforementioned generic prerequisites, it is not unlikely that a given behavior will have a prerequisite unique to that behavior or to a particular group of behaviors. For example, maladaptive behaviors often function as solutions to student problems. Students continually rely on "solutions" that are maladaptive because they have difficulty perceiving any alternatives. If someone teases you, the best solution is to fight them. If you can't get what you want, the best solution is to have a tantrum. These students need to be able to perceive alternatives such as the target behavior as viable solutions to their problems.

Environmental Prerequisites

Sometimes assessment results suggest that a student has all of the personal prerequisites necessary to engage in a target behavior, but the student fails to engage in that behavior in the classroom. It is also possible that a student lacking one or more personal prerequisites may have difficulty remediating that deficit because an environmental prerequisite is lacking. Remember Bandura's (1974, 1977, 1986) theory of reciprocal determinism: Human behavior is the result of reciprocal influences between the personal variables (internal) of the individual, the environment (external) in which the behavior occurs, and the behavior itself.

For example, a student might have difficulty responding assertively to peer teasing because the environment in which the teasing occurs lacks one or more of the following prerequisites.

1. *Ample opportunity* to develop *competence* at being assertive. Whenever teasing occurs in the classroom and the teacher is aware of it, she tries to intervene before a stu-

dent has an opportunity to respond. She always assumes the worst—that the student will respond aggressively. Thus, the target student has few opportunities to practice the assertive behavior he has been taught in his social skills lessons.

2. *Sufficient reinforcement* to *motivate* the student to be assertive. When the student does respond assertively, the teacher fails to acknowledge his behavior. Meanwhile, most of his peers are immune to his assertiveness because they view it as a weakness and tease (or mimic) him ("Oh. Stop that. I don't like that," spoken in a young child's voice). In other words, on those rare occasions when the student is assertive, his behavior is either ignored by the teacher or punished by the peer group. In either case, his assertive behavior is weakened (via extinction and punishment).

3. *Appropriate models* to develop the *expectation* and *competence* prerequisites. The teacher, by being excessively critical of his students, models behavior very similar to the teasing behavior of his students. He also responds to any question of his authority by being aggressive and punitive instead of being assertive. His students also model aggressive behavior through name calling, shaming, and disapproving of others.

4. *Positive setting events* to help better maintain emotional *self-control*. The teacher unwittingly sets up an environment ripe for teasing by requiring the student and his peers, all of whom have learning problems, to perform difficult tasks in front of the class (e.g., reading orally, doing work at the blackboard, answering questions). Because there is ample opportunity for failure, these tasks function as negative setting events in producing frustration, anxiety, and anger, all of which contribute to the aggressive teasing behavior.

Although environmental prerequisites are as important as personal prerequisites in evaluating behavior problems, lack of time (yours) and lack of space (mine) preclude my covering both prerequisites in detail in this program. Besides, you should be able to identify many of the environmental prerequisite deficits through the traditional FBA. My objective here is to simply make you aware of the interaction between the environmental and personal prerequisites that influence behavior. To that end, I have provided a list of generic environmental prerequisites in Table 1.2.

Evaluation

Once the maladaptive and target behaviors have been identified and prerequisites listed, the third step in Beyond

FA is to determine whether or not your student lacks any of the prerequisites. There are two ways to do this: without assessments and with assessments.

Without Assessments

First try to determine the status of a prerequisite informally before you turn to a formal assessment. If you have a history with the target student, it is often possible to decide whether or not she has the prerequisite without having to assess it. Although the indicators listed below are not foolproof, they should help you in your decision making. If you decide that your student has a given prerequisite without using an assessment, I recommend that you write the indicator (see below) in the "Status" column on the Beyond FA worksheet so that other individuals will know what you are basing your decision on. *Important:* If you do err in making a decision without using an assessment, it is always best to err on the conservative side. In other words, it is better to decide that your student does *not* have a prerequisite without testing for it rather than deciding that he does have it.

1. Expectation

(a) *Yes—the student understands what he is expected to do if:* He has told you *in his own words on more than one occasion* what behavior is expected of him and/or you have observed the student apply the rule. For example, if he is engaging in the maladaptive behavior and knows you are watching him, and he stops what he is doing and starts engaging in the target behavior, he probably understands what behaviors he should and should not be engaging in.

(b) *No—the student does not understand what he is expected to do if:* You already asked him (in the past) what the expectation (rule behavior) is and he cannot tell you in his own words.

2. Self-Awareness

(a) *Yes—the student is aware of her behavior if:* You have, on more than one occasion, observed her stop herself from engaging in the maladaptive behavior without any feedback from others. This is usually a good indication that she is aware enough to provide her own feedback.

(b) *No—the student is not aware of her behavior if:* She does not change her behavior unless someone brings it to her attention. The behavior may be so ingrained that she can't provide her own feedback. It could also be that she becomes so emotionally upset that her level of awareness is inhibited or she is very stubborn

Table 1.2
Generic Environmental Prerequisites (Necessary for Students to Gain Personal Prerequisites and/or Engage in Target Behaviors)

1. *Effective Instruction*

    The teacher effectively communicates the rule behavior to all students by clearly stating the rule and consistently enforcing it (necessary to gain the *expectation* prerequisite).

    Assess through Direct Observation (self-monitoring when appropriate)

    Rule behavior(s) posted in classroom?
    Verbal reminders provided when necessary?
    Rule behavior(s) consistently enforced?
    Students periodically questioned re rule behavior(s)?

    The teacher provides effective instruction in how to engage in the target behavior (necessary to gain the *competence* prerequisite).

    Assess through Teacher Interview and/or Direct Observation

    Direct instruction provided in specific social and academic behaviors? How often?
    Data collected re efficacy of instruction?

2. *Appropriate Models*

    The teacher and the peer group provide appropriate models of the target behaviors (necessary to gain *expectation* and *competence* prerequisites).

    Assess through Direct Observation

3. *Consistent Feedback*

    The teacher (and/or the peer group) cues students *in a neutral manner* when the student engages in appropriate and inappropriate behavior (necessary to gain *self-awareness*).

    Assess through Direct Observation (self-monitoring if appropriate)

4. *Sufficient Reinforcement*

    The teacher (and/or the peer group) appropriately and consistently consequates students when they engage in maladaptive and target behaviors (necessary to gain the *motivation* prerequisite).

    Assess through Direct Observation (self-monitoring when appropriate)

    The teacher, either through verbal or physical behavior, reinforces rational thinking communicated by students (necessary to gain the *beliefs* prerequisite).

    Assess through Teacher Interview and/or Direct Observation (self-monitoring when appropriate)

5. *Ample Opportunity*

    The environment provides students with enough opportunities to practice engaging in the target behavior (necessary to gain *competence*).

    Assess through Direct Observation (self-monitoring if appropriate)

6. *Positive Setting Events*

    The teacher (and school) create school environments conducive for engaging in target behaviors (necessary to gain the *self-control* prerequisite).

    Assess through Teacher Interview and/or Direct Observation

    Students on medication are taking same?
    Students requiring hearing or vision aids are using same?
    Students requiring learning aids (e.g., tutors, curriculum adaptations) are provided with and using same?

(i.e., she knows what she is doing as she does it but doesn't care or is very driven by her beliefs, feelings). In this case, it is best that you assess her.

3. Self-Control

(a) *Yes—the student is able to control his behavior if:* You have observed the student stop himself from engaging in the maladaptive behavior. If he does this without external feedback, this means he probably has self-awareness *as well as* self-control. If he stops himself only after being given feedback, you can assume that he has self-control but not necessarily self-awareness. Another indicator that he has self-control is if you have observed him engage in the maladaptive behavior on a self-selective basis (e.g., he only responds aggressively to peer provocation when the peers are same size or smaller; does not respond aggressively to provocation from older or larger peers).

(b) *No—the student is not able to control his behavior if:* You have observed the student engage in the maladaptive behavior even when it is obvious to him that he will be physically hurt or punished (e.g., will attack peers of any size or age or behave in similar manner with all adults). This can be indicative of an anger management problem and/or poor impulse control. Another indicator is that you have observed obvious signs of problematic emotionality (e.g., anger, anxiety, depression) or impulsivity in the student or the student has already been diagnosed by a reliable source as having a biophysical, sensory, or neurological impairment that makes it difficult for him to engage in the target behavior.

4. Competence

(a) *Yes—the student knows how to engage in the target behavior if:* You have observed her *on more than one occasion* correctly engaging in the target behavior (e.g., you have seen her acting assertively or attending to the task or accessing attention correctly). It is not enough that she can explain how she is supposed to act; she needs to actually do it.

(b) *No—the student (probably) does not know how to engage in the target behavior if:* You have seen her consistently engage in the target behavior incorrectly or not at all.

5. Motivation

(a) *Yes—the student considers the consequences of the target behavior more rewarding or less aversive than the*

consequences of the maladaptive behavior if: You have observed the student engaging in other behaviors for the same consequences. At least you know that the consequences work sometimes. This doesn't necessarily mean they will work for this particular behavior.

(b) *No—the student does not consider the consequences of the target behavior more rewarding or less aversive than the consequences of the maladaptive behavior if:* You already know that the consequences of the target behavior are not as strong as the consequences of the maladaptive behavior.

6. Beliefs

Because you can't read minds, you will have to rely on the student's verbal behavior to decide about this prerequisite. Ask yourself if the student's verbal behavior suggests what he thinks about school, teachers, peers, and, most importantly, the maladaptive and target behaviors. For example, students who *typically* say things like, "This is too hard. I'll never be able to do it," "It's all his (your) fault. He (she) made me do it," "I can't help it," or "That won't work" may be endorsing an external locus of control or low self-efficacy belief. I recommend that you always use an assessment to determine the status of this prerequisite.

With Assessments

If you have any doubt about the status of a prerequisite, you need to conduct an assessment. For the most part, the type of assessment used in Beyond FA may be defined as behavioral assessment—"the most important aspects of [which] are its emphasis on using a variety of procedures and the link between assessment and intervention" (Breen & Fiedler, 1996, p. 4). The variety of procedures used in behavioral assessment, many of which are employed in Beyond FA, include the direct observation of student (and adult) behavior in naturalistic (classroom) and analogue (contrived) settings; role playing; student, teacher, and parent interviews; self-report measures; and rating scales and checklists. Are these assessment procedures valid? Unlike many standardized pencil-and-paper measures such as tests of intellect and achievement, they may not have statistical evidence of reliability or validity. This does not mean that they are not valid. If you adhere to both the general recommendations below and the specific directions that follow each worksheet, you will greatly enhance the probability of valid assessment.

You have the option of using the assessments provided for you in Beyond FA. They are written specifically for a given maladaptive/target behavior and may be found in

Section 3, Worksheet/Assessment Methods and Materials (with the exception of the beliefs assessments, which are found in Appendix A). You also have the option of using an alternative assessment, listed in Appendix C. I do recommend that, whenever possible, you use *both* the assessment provided in the Worksheet/Assessment Methods and Materials section *and* one of the alternative assessments in Appendix C to corroborate your findings. More on this later.

The following section provides some *general*, but important, information regarding the assessments provided in Beyond FA. *Please read it before administering any of the assessments.*

1. If your student refuses to cooperate on any assessment and/or you have reason to suspect the validity of his responses, you have three options: (a) You can try using the same assessment again later; (b) you can try using an alternative assessment now or later; or (c) you can assume that the student does not have the prerequisite in question and act accordingly (i.e., follow through with the intervention for that prerequisite). If you choose the latter, you will soon find out whether or not he has the prerequisite when you implement the intervention. If he does have the prerequisite, you can always stop the intervention without having wasted much time or frustrated the student. On the other hand, if you assume he has the prerequisite when he actually doesn't, you not only can waste more time, but you can also set both of you up for failure and frustration, making it less likely that your student will cooperate in future efforts.

2. Although the *self-awareness* prerequisite is essential for all of the behaviors covered in this program, an obvious ethical concern related to the testing of this prerequisite must be considered. The most logical and probably most valid method of assessing the student's self-awareness (i.e., she knows what she is doing *when she is doing it*) is for the student and the teacher to simultaneously, but separately, monitor the frequency of the student's behavior in the naturalistic setting of the classroom and then compare their data. Ideally, the student should monitor her behavior on her own (i.e., without any external cues). However, a problem arises when the behavior the student is supposed to monitor is potentially dangerous or disruptive. For example, when the target student engages in physically aggressive behavior, the teacher has to intervene as quickly as possible so that no one gets hurt. Unfortunately, the act of intervening cues the target student so that she becomes aware of her behavior. The primary objective of this assessment is to determine whether or not *the student can cue herself*. When she is cued by the teacher, the objective changes from measuring the student's awareness of her behavior to measuring the teacher's awareness

of it. In such a case, the ethical concerns must override concerns about validity. I therefore recommend the following: (a) Do not function as both the observer (data collector) and participant in the classroom action; if you think it will work, have your assistant collect data or participate in the classroom action while you collect data; and/or (b) you might use a different (but less valid) assessment to measure your student's awareness; one procedure might be for you to interview the student *at the end of a given period of time* to establish her awareness of the behavior instead of having her collect data *as it happens*; this way, you don't have to worry so much about cueing her when you need to intervene; for example, let's say you monitor her aggressive behavior for a 30-minute period; at the end of the 30 minutes, ask her how many times *she thinks* she engaged in the maladaptive behavior and the target (fair-pair) behavior and compare her impression with the behavioral data you collected; this is not the best way to assess her awareness, but it may be safer for all concerned and will give you some indication of how aware of her behavior she is.

3. Always try to take the issue of diversity into account. For example, if English is the student's second language, you may need someone fluent in the student's first language to conduct the assessments. In addition to language, you need to consider culture. Pay particular attention to the *expectation* prerequisite. Are your expectations or the school's expectations compatible with the student's cultural background? You should also consider the *motivation* and *beliefs* prerequisites. Are the consequences of student behavior that are rewarding to the majority culture (White/Anglo/Christian) also rewarding to the minority culture the target student comes from? Are the belief systems compatible? To answer these questions, you can interview other students and/or adults who come from the same cultural background as the target student. An excellent resource on diversity and behavior problems is *Instruction in a Diverse Society*, by Herbert Grossman (1995).

4. If your student has difficulty responding to any assessment utilizing a supply-response format (where she *produces the answer* from memory), try switching to a select-response format (where she *identifies the answer* from a group of answers). This way, all she has to do is answer "yes" or "no," give one- or two-word responses, or simply nod or shake her head. On the other hand, if the student has difficulty with receptive language (e.g., reading deficit), try having her listen to the question(s) instead of reading them. Again, be flexible and don't hesitate to improvise when necessary.

5. Try to impress upon your student the importance of responding honestly (i.e., how he really feels), especially

on the subjective measures used in assessing the *motivation* and *beliefs* prerequisites. Make sure he knows he will not be penalized in any way for his responses and be sure that you stick to your promise. Remember that your objective is to find out why the student behaves the way he does and not to lecture. You are testing now, not teaching. If you have any reason to believe that your student may not respond honestly to an assessment in your presence, let him complete it on his own or in the presence of a third party.

6. Always make sure that the student understands the directions for an assessment. Have her paraphrase them (not simply repeat them) before she takes it.

7. If you object to the criterion for acceptable performance for any of the prerequisites, you may adjust them if you like, *but remember*, the easier you make it for your student to "pass" an assessment, the less confidence you can have in the results. If you want to substitute your own time or accuracy criteria for mine, here is the procedure I recommend you follow: (a) Identify a small sample of students ($N = 2$ or 3) that *you already know* have the prerequisite in question (let's refer to them as "exemplars"); (b) give the exemplars in your sample the prerequisite assessment; and (c) use their median score (i.e., middle score) as the criterion for the student(s) you have doubts about. For example, if you think a student should have more than 10 seconds to respond in the *expectation* assessment, use the median time it took the exemplars to respond. If two of them took 15 seconds and a third took 10 seconds, the median time is 15 seconds. If you are satisfied with this, use it.

8. One thing you can do to improve the validity of your assessment results is to give an assessment more than once. When you are using direct observation of the student's behavior, collect more than one sample. A minimum of 3 days is suggested. This is also necessary when you are assessing the *motivation* and *beliefs* prerequisites. Your student's mood at the time you assess her on either of these assessments can influence her responses. This is especially true of students with emotional and/or behavioral disabilities. To control for mood, I suggest you use the test–retest method with at least a 24-hour latency between trials. Another way to improve validity is to use more than one assessment for a given prerequisite. As I have already mentioned, there are several alternative assessments listed in Appendix C that you may wish to use *in addition to* those I have provided for you.

Assessments

This section describes the assessment methods and materials you will be using to assess each of the prerequisites. It is intended to serve as an introduction and a supplement to the specific assessment instructions that follow each of the Beyond FA worksheets. It is important that you read this material before you administer any of the assessments.

1. Expectation

The *objective* of this assessment is to determine whether or not the target student understands what behavior is expected of him. The assessment *method* used is open-ended interview: Ask the student to tell you in his own words what he is supposed to do. Being able to recite the rule behavior verbatim does not necessarily mean that the student understands it. It simply means that he has memorized it. Always preface your question with, "Tell me in your own words." Samples of questions specific to each of the 10 target behaviors can be found after each of the worksheets.

If your student has an expressive language problem, an *alternative* assessment is to ask him to look around the room and name the students in the class who are, *at that moment,* following and not following the rule(s). If he doesn't know their names, point to a student and say, "Is she following the rule?" He should simply answer "yes" or "no" or nod or shake his head. Obviously, you should do this without alerting the other students so that they don't confuse the target student by changing their behavior.

Another alternative is to have the student *show you* what he is and is not supposed to do. For example, if the student usually calls out without raising his hand, say, "Show me what you are supposed to do to get my attention." (student should raise hand and wait). Then say, "Now show me what you are *not* supposed to do to get my attention" (student should call out without raising hand or raise hand and call out). If you use a supply-response format where the student is required to *produce* the response, one trial testing should suffice. He either can do it or he can't. If a select-response format is used and the student has to *identify* the correct response from several possible, he should be required to respond correctly on several trials to control for guessing. Whether you use a supply-response or select-response format, the student should answer correctly immediately and with little or no prompting.

2. Self-Awareness

The *objective* of the assessment is to determine whether or not the target student knows what she is doing when she is doing it. The *method* used to assess this is direct observation of behavior in a naturalistic (i.e., classroom) setting, which I refer to as *simultaneous monitoring*. You and the target student simultaneously, but separately, monitor her behavior and compare data. You will know what the student is doing when she does it because it is observable and you are watching her. You will know when the student is off task because you will see her look away from her work. Unfortunately, the student may be so preoccupied by whatever is going on in the environment (or in her head) that she might not realize she is off task. It logically follows that if the student's self-awareness data are the same or similar to yours, she probably has this prerequisite.

There are two ways to conduct simultaneous monitoring: the gross method and the precise method. Let's examine the gross method first. Assume both you and the student are monitoring her talk-out and hand-raising behavior. When the student shouts out or when she raises her hand and waits, both you and the student record it separately. She doesn't see what you are marking and you don't see what she is marking. At the end of the monitoring period, each of you simply totals the number of maladaptive and target behaviors you recorded. Let's say that you observed the student shouting out 10 times and raising her hand and waiting only twice. The student, meanwhile, recorded only five talk-outs and two times when she raised her hand. *Using the maladaptive behavior data,* you calculate the percentage of agreement between your data and the student's data by dividing the higher number (10) into the lower number (5) to get .50 and then multiply by 100 to get 50%. This is the percentage of agreement between your data and the student's data with regard to the maladaptive behavior (see Figure 1.3). Given that an *acceptable percentage of agreement is at least 80%* (see Alberto & Troutman, 1995, p. 136), the student is probably not as aware of her shouting-out behavior as she should be. You might say, "Wait. If we *use the target behavior data,* there is 100% agreement between us; two divided into two = 1 × 100 = 100%." Remember that we said that neither of you watches the other to see what you recorded.

Let's suppose that on each of the two separate occasions when you recorded a talk-out, the student recorded a hand-raise. This means that even though you each recorded a total of two hand raises, because they were recorded at different times, your totals really don't agree at all. This is why the first method of calculating interobserver agreement is sometimes referred to as the "gross" method (Alberto & Troutman, p. 135).

The more precise (albeit less simple) method of simultaneous monitoring is sometimes referred to in the literature as the "point-by-point agreement ratio" (Malott, Whaley, & Malott, 1997, p. 439). It requires that you and your student record your data in a series of boxes one box at a time *and in the same sequential order.* For example, as Figure 1.4 shows, the first behavior you observe is a *talk-out* and you record it as such in your first box on the left. At the same time, your student records the same behavior as a *hand raise-and-wait* in her first box. The next behavior you observe is another talk-out, which you record in your second box, while the student again records it as a hand raise-and-wait in her second box. This routine continues until all of the boxes on each of your forms are filled. As you look at Figure 1.4, notice that if you simply count the number of talk-outs (0) each of you recorded (5 and 7), the percentage of agreement between you and the student is 71% (i.e., 5 divided by 7 × 100). Not bad. Now let's see how the data compare when you use the point-by-point agreement ratio. Beginning with your first box and the student's first box, you label all of the agrees and disagrees between your data and her data in left-to-right sequence. You then take the total number of agrees and disagrees (2 + 8 = 10) and divide it into the total number of agrees (2/10 = .20). Multiply this by 100 and you get your percentage of agreement (20%). As you can see, the agreement between your two sets of data is much less than you thought.

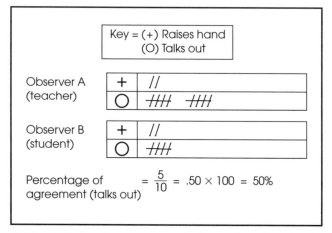

Figure 1.3. Simultaneous monitoring using the simple ("gross") method.

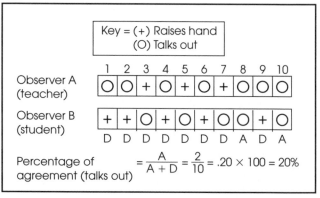

Figure 1.4. Simultaneous monitoring using the more precise (point-by-point agreement ratio) method. *Note.* D = disagreement between teacher and student; A = agreement between teacher and student.

Specific instructions for using the gross method of simultaneous monitoring are provided after each of the Beyond FA worksheets, whereas the basic instructions for using the point-by-point agreement ratio are listed below. Depending on your understanding of the methodology, the amount of time you have, and how unsure you are about the student's self-awareness, you have the option of using either method. However, if you do choose the gross method, I recommend that you conduct the simultaneous monitoring for *at least* three separate trials and use 90% (rather than 80%) as the criterion for agreement. You can probably get away with three or fewer trials using the point-by-point method with a criterion of 80% for agreement.

To use the point-by-point agreement ratio do the following:

1. Draw a number of boxes on your recording form. The number may be determined by the length of the monitoring interval and/or an estimate of the number of student behaviors that you expect to occur. Try to use at least 10 boxes.

2. Explain to the student what you want her to do (see below).

3. Each time you observe the student engaging in the behavior you are monitoring, record a mark in one of the boxes beginning with the first box on the left and moving in a left-to-right sequence.

4. You may check the student's monitoring *once*. Look to see if she has recorded the behavior *in the correct box*. If yes, continue recording without further checking on the student. If no, tell the student to put the mark in the first box on the left and remind her to record in each box in a left-to-right sequence. If you notice that the student recorded the wrong mark in the correct box, do not correct her.

5. When all of the boxes *on your sheet* have been filled, stop recording and compare your data with the student's data to compute the percentage of interobserver agreement (see Figure 1.4). If the student left one or more boxes empty, count these as disagrees.

3. Self-Control

Your *objective* here is to determine whether or not there is a biophysical or emotional condition, currently not under the student's control, which makes it difficult for her to engage in the fair-pair target behavior. There are several *methods* you may use to assess this prerequisite. The possible biophysical and emotional conditions that might contribute to each of the 10 maladaptive behaviors are listed on each Beyond FA worksheet in the "Assessment"

column. Biophysical factors such as sensory impairment, medication or side effects of medication, seizure activity, and hyperactivity and distractibility associated with attention-deficit/hyperactivity disorder (ADHD) are relatively easy to assess. They are either present or not present and can be found by perusing the student's cumulative record folder or health history, interviewing family members about the student's behavior outside of school (e.g., "Has the subject ever been diagnosed with a hearing or vision loss? Does he take medication? What for? Any side effects? Any evidence of seizure activity? Has he ever been diagnosed as ADHD? When? By whom? On what basis?"), and/or having the school nurse or speech pathologist examine the student.

Emotional factors such as depression, anger, anxiety, and impulsivity (which is actually more of a temperament trait or behavioral style than an emotion) are harder to assess because they can vary by frequency or intensity and need to be compared to the "norm." The assessment *method* recommended is direct observation in a naturalistic setting (e.g., the classroom), which I refer to as "peer comparison monitoring." For example, when you measure the frequency of the target student's anxiety and compare the results with the behavior of peers you know are anxious and with peers you know are not anxious, which group does she resemble the most? Table 1.3 lists a number of the behavioral correlates or observable signs of anger, anxiety, depression, and impulsivity. Use these signs when you conduct your peer comparison monitoring.

Instructions for peer comparison assessment specific to each prerequisite are provided following each worksheet. If possible, try to have another person monitor the target student and her peers in exactly the same manner as you. After each trial, you can calculate interobserver agreement using either the point-by-point procedure or by simply dividing the larger number into the smaller number. Having two observers monitoring the same thing at the same time helps insure that the data you collect are reliable. I suggest that in addition to the peer comparison assessment described above, you also use one of the alternative assessments listed in Appendix C.

4. Competence

The *objective* of this assessment is to determine whether or not your student knows how to engage in the target behavior. The *method* of assessment is the *role play test*, in which he is asked to demonstrate the target behavior in a number of situations approximating those he actually experiences in the school setting. These role play tests are located immediately following the Beyond FA worksheets. There are also some pencil-and-paper social skills

Table 1.3

Behavioral Correlates of Emotional States That Typically Contribute to Maladaptive Behavior

Anger

heightened frequency or intensity of aggressive behavior (e.g., punching, slapping, pushing, kicking, spitting, cursing, yelling, teasing, making threats)

temper tantrums

changes in speech (e.g., disfluencies) or quality and tone of voice (e.g., shrill or low)

facial expressions (looks angry)

verbalizations ("I'm angry!")

movement of extremities (e.g., arm and hand waving)

gestures and posture (e.g., hand banging, table banging, fist clenching, hands on hips, arms folded across chest)

Anxiety

speech disturbances/speech disfluencies (e.g., corrections, "ahs," "uhs," mispronunciations, incomplete words)

quality and tone of voice (e.g., shrill or low)

rate of speech (e.g., marked acceleration or deceleration)

synchrony between verbal and nonverbal behaviors (occur simultaneously)

verbalizations (e.g., "This is scary.")

movement (e.g., pacing back and forth)

orientation of eyes or head (e.g., changes frequently)

self-manipulations (e.g., touching face, wringing hands)

facial expressions (looks scared or anxious)

gestures and posture (e.g., "defensive" movements of hands)

number of questions asked regarding performance or security of individual increases

Depression

slowed rate of speech

number of verbal behaviors directed toward others (decreases)

verbalizations (e.g., "This is hopeless.")

decreased range of interactions with others

number of positive reactions versus negative reactions

action latency—speed with which the student responds to another's reaction is slow

activity level (decreases)

voice volume (decreases)

eye contact (less)

affect—facial expression (flat or sad)

head aversions (head oriented away from person speaking)

smiling (limited)

Impulsivity

acts without reflecting on his or her actions (student shows sincere remorse after engaging in maladaptive behavior)

starts tasks before getting all directions/relevant information from teacher

action latency—speed with which student responds to another's reaction is quick

tendency to perseverate on tasks with select-response format (selects same answer over and over again)

manifests obvious impatience when required to wait

measures you might want to use instead of the role play tests or in combination with them. These are listed in Appendix C.

Not all of the competencies assessed are social skills. For example, the competency required in Target Behavior 1 is "has skills and knowledge necessary to work on assigned tasks without supervision." Your objective for this prerequisite is to determine whether or not your student has all of the skills and knowledge required to successfully work on the tasks you assign him. For example, if you assign him the task of putting a puzzle together, he should be able to pick up puzzle pieces and correctly place them together. If you assign him the task of answering questions at the end of chapter in a science text, he should be able to read for comprehension, form answers in his mind, and write them out. If he can't perform these tasks successfully, chances are he will require close supervision to stay on task. A good method for assessing such skill and knowledge competencies is curriculum-based assessment. The idea is simple but logical. If you want to see whether or not your student has mastered the curriculum you are teaching him, you should use the very same tasks he is required to perform on a daily basis in you class as the items for your assessment. In other words, if your student requires constant supervision to perform Task A, sit down with him and see whether or not he can perform Task A while supervised. If he can, this means that his problem is probably a lack of motivation and you need to "sweeten" the consequences for completing tasks. If he can't perform Task A, even when supervised, his problem is more likely to be a lack of competence, and you need to conduct a curriculum-based assessment to determine the student's true level of functioning and change the tasks you assign him. An excellent resource on curriculum-based assessment is *Curriculum-Based Evaluation: Teaching and Decision Making*, by Howell, Fox, and Morehead (1993).

5. Motivation

There are actually two *objectives* of this assessment: to determine (a) whether or not the student knows the consequences of engaging in the maladaptive and target behaviors and (b) how she feels about (values) them. The *method* for determining the first objective is to simply ask the student what happens when she engages in the maladaptive behavior and in the target behavior. If she can't supply the correct answer(s), have her select the answer(s) from a list of consequences you provide her. For example, "When you do your work on your own without reminders, which of the following things happens? (Answer yes or no): You are given more work to do. You are given ____ points. You get to do whatever you want. You get praise

from your teacher(s)." Repeat the same process to determine whether or not the student knows the consequences of needing supervision to get her work done.

I should mention here that it is essential to establish the consistency of the teacher in providing consequences. If the teacher has used different consequences or presented them inconsistently, it will be difficult for the student to learn what the consequences of her behavior are. Assuming she does know the consequences of her behavior, use the cue-sort method (Howell et al., 1993; Stephenson, 1980) to determine which of these consequences the student considers pleasing and which she considers aversive. Specific instructions for the cue-sort method are provided after each worksheet. *Remember:* It is not enough to determine how the student feels about each consequence; you want to know how she feels about each *relative to the others*. This is why you have her sort the consequences into those she likes and those she doesn't like. An *alternative* or complementary assessment is to have her *rank* the consequences according to likes and dislikes from most to least liked. Ideally, the consequences of the fair-pair target behavior will be ranked higher than those of the maladaptive behavior.

6. Beliefs

The *objective* of this assessment is to determine whether or not the target student holds any beliefs that might be incompatible with the target behavior. The *method* for assessing this prerequisite is a pencil-and-paper beliefs assessment. These assessments can be found in Appendix A. A description of the construction and validation process for the beliefs assessments used in Beyond FA appears below. Information regarding the administration and scoring of the beliefs assessments can also be found in Appendix A.

Construction and Validation of the Beliefs Assessments

1. A description of a hypothetical student maladaptive behavior was written.

2. On the basis of this description, a number of irrational beliefs thought to be incompatible with the target behavior were generated.

3. For each irrational belief, a rational belief thought to be compatible with the target behavior was written.

4. The description of the hypothetical student and his maladaptive behavior and all of the irrational and rational beliefs were used to develop the survey shown in Figure 1.5.

Name _____ **Date** _____

Directions: Which of the 18 beliefs stated on the following pages do you think are most typical of a *student who is extremely sensitive to criticism from adults?* When criticized by teachers (i.e., when they point out a mistake or something he or she is doing wrong and/or attempt to correct him or her), this student gets visibly upset and refuses to cooperate (i.e., gives up, refuses to try the task again, or refuses to respond altogether). Please indicate *how typical* each belief is by marking (circle) the descriptor underneath each belief.

Descriptor Key:

Very Typical . . . . the student *definitely believes* this

Somewhat Typical . . . . . . the student *probably believes* this

Less Typical . . . . the student *probably does not believe* this

Atypical . . . . the student *definitely does not believe* this

Don't Know . . . . not enough information given about the student to make a decision about whether or not the student believes this

If you are not satisfied with the wording of a statement, please feel free to change it. Also, feel free to make comments regarding any of the items.

1. Nobody's perfect.
   Very Typical　　　*Somewhat Typical*　　　*Less Typical*　　　*Atypical*　　　*Don't Know*

2. Everyone makes mistakes.
   Very Typical　　　*Somewhat Typical*　　　*Less Typical*　　　*Atypical*　　　*Don't Know*

3. My teachers like it when I'm wrong.
   Very Typical　　　*Somewhat Typical*　　　*Less Typical*　　　*Atypical*　　　*Don't Know*

4. I'm a failure.
   Very Typical　　　*Somewhat Typical*　　　*Less Typical*　　　*Atypical*　　　*Don't Know*

5. What you think about yourself is more important than what others think about you.
   Very Typical　　　*Somewhat Typical*　　　*Less Typical*　　　*Atypical*　　　*Don't Know*

6. I never make mistakes.
   Very Typical　　　*Somewhat Typical*　　　*Less Typical*　　　*Atypical*　　　*Don't Know*

7. You learn by your mistakes.
   Very Typical　　　*Somewhat Typical*　　　*Less Typical*　　　*Atypical*　　　*Don't Know*

8. Mistakes are always bad.
   Very Typical　　　*Somewhat Typical*　　　*Less Typical*　　　*Atypical*　　　*Don't Know*

9. I never do anything right.
   Very Typical　　　*Somewhat Typical*　　　*Less Typical*　　　*Atypical*　　　*Don't Know*

10. If at first you don't succeed, try, try again.
    Very Typical　　　*Somewhat Typical*　　　*Less Typical*　　　*Atypical*　　　*Don't Know*

Figure 1.5. Validation edition of beliefs assessment survey. From *Beyond Behavior Modification* (3rd ed., pp. 416–417), by Joseph S. Kaplan with Jane Carter, 1995, Austin, TX: PRO-ED. Copyright 1995 by PRO-ED. Reprinted with permission.

11. What others think or say about you is more important than what you think about yourself.
    Very Typical   *Somewhat Typical*   *Less Typical*   *Atypical*   *Don't Know*

12. I must be stupid if I make mistakes.
    Very Typical   *Somewhat Typical*   *Less Typical*   *Atypical*   *Don't Know*

13. It's my teachers' job to tell me when I'm wrong.
    Very Typical   *Somewhat Typical*   *Less Typical*   *Atypical*   *Don't Know*

14. It's OK to make mistakes.
    Very Typical   *Somewhat Typical*   *Less Typical*   *Atypical*   *Don't Know*

15. You can fail at something and still be a good person.
    Very Typical   *Somewhat Typical*   *Less Typical*   *Atypical*   *Don't Know*

16. I must be good at everything I do and it's awful if I'm not.
    Very Typical   *Somewhat Typical*   *Less Typical*   *Atypical*   *Don't Know*

17. I'm good at lots of things.
    Very Typical   *Somewhat Typical*   *Less Typical*   *Atypical*   *Don't Know*

18. If at first you don't succeed, it's best to give up so you won't be disappointed anymore.
    Very Typical   *Somewhat Typical*   *Less Typical*   *Atypical*   *Don't Know*

Figure 1.5. *Continued.*

5. The survey was completed by an individual with expertise in the areas of rational emotive behavior therapy for children and emotional and behavioral disabilities.

6. Items on the survey marked "very typical" and "atypical" were included in the final form of the beliefs assessment. Items marked "somewhat typical" and "don't know" were not included in the final form.

7. Distractor items, having nothing to do with the maladaptive behavior, were generated and added to the final form along with directions to the subject and answer key and directions for scoring the examiner.

This section has provided introductory and supplementary information about the assessment of each of the personal prerequisites. Specific assessment instructions follow each of the Beyond FA worksheets.

Interpretation

The fourth and final step in Beyond FA is interpreting the results of the evaluation. This involves identifying the pre-requisites the student lacks, writing a performance objective for each, and identifying an intervention strategy to remediate the prerequisite deficit. Performance objectives complete with criteria for acceptable performance (CAP) for each of the prerequisites and for each of the target behaviors covered in Beyond FA may be found in Appendix B. Recommendations for intervention strategies are described in Section 4, "Interventions," and in Appendix C.

Special Considerations

If it turns out that your student is lacking more than one prerequisite, but you want to implement one intervention at a time, I suggest you begin with the easiest intervention to implement. Direct instruction of the *expectation* prerequisite is easy. Environmental interventions that require changes in the physical environment (e.g., changing seating arrangements in the classroom) are also relatively easy. Some medical interventions, such as getting the student a pair of reading glasses or changing the dosage of his asthma medication, can be relatively easy to implement. Behavior modification interventions can be easy if you have had experience using them and all you need to do is make changes in reinforcers and/or reinforcement schedules. Remedial interventions, especially where academic or social skill instruction is required, are harder to implement, primarily because they take longer than the others to produce results in the student's maladaptive behavior.

The hardest interventions to implement are the cognitive and cognitive-behavioral interventions such as teaching problem solving, cognitive restructuring, self-instructional training, and stress inoculation. Unfortunately, these are often the most needed interventions, especially when intense, counterproductive emotions are involved. Self-monitoring can probably fit in anywhere in this hierarchy of interventions, but it is essential for success in managing one's emotions since self-awareness is a critical component in this type of intervention.

Occasionally, you may finish the evaluation portion of Beyond FA and determine that your student has all of the prerequisites he needs to engage in the target behavior. In this case, if you decided that your student has any of the prerequisites without using an assessment, I would suggest that you assess these prerequisites just to be on the safe side. You might also reassess the prerequisites you assessed earlier, just to make sure you were right the first time. If a second go-round yields the same results, you might consider one or two prerequisites that are *unique* to the target behavior and have not been assessed.

If you find that your student does in fact have all of the personal prerequisites but still does not engage in the target behavior, consider if any of the environmental prerequisites are lacking. Refer to Table 1.2 for a list of generic environmental prerequisites along with recommended assessments.

Using Beyond FA

Beyond FA is easy to use. Follow the steps outlined below.

▶ **Step 1** Scan the descriptions of maladaptive behaviors beginning on page 4 of this book until you find the behavior you want to work on.

▶ **Step 2** Consult the table of contents to select the worksheet for the behavior you have chosen to work on. Make a copy of the worksheet, and then fill out the information at the top of the worksheet (student, evaluator, and date). See Figure 2.1 for a sample completed worksheet. Please note that each worksheet consists of two pages, and that the two pages should be placed side-by-side after copying for ease in completing the worksheet. Each row aligns across the two pages.

▶ **Step 3** Locate the "Prerequisites" column on the worksheet, read each, and ask yourself if there is any evidence that the target student has the prerequisite.

If you *already know* the student has a *prerequisite* without completing an assessment, place a check mark in the "Y" box under the "Status" column next to that prerequisite. Be sure to write a brief statement (e.g., "I have seen him do this on several occasions") under the "Y" box to support your response. See Figure 2.1.

If you *already know* the student does not have a *prerequisite* without an assessment, place a check mark in the "N" box under the "Status" column. See Figure 2.1.

If you are not sure if the student has the *prerequisite*, place a check mark in the "?" box under the "Status" column next to the prerequisite.

Do this for each of the six (or seven) prerequisites. Again, refer to Figure 2.1.

▶ **Step 4** Step 4 should be completed only if one or more of the prerequisites are in doubt. Use the information provided in the "Assessment" column to locate the assessment instructions and materials. Complete the assessment(s) and write the results in the "Results" column on the worksheet. See Figure 2.1.

Important: If the results of an assessment indicate that the student has the prerequisite, go back to the "Status" column and change the "?" to "Y." See Figure 2.1.

If the results indicate that the student does *not* have the prerequisite, change the "?" to "N" and follow Step 5 below. See Figure 2.1.

▶ **Step 5** Complete a behavioral intervention plan (BIP) using the information from your evaluation. A sample BIP is provided in Figure 2.2. For each prerequisite the student is lacking ("N"), write a performance objective (refer to Appendix B) in the "Objective" column. Then use the information provided in the "Intervention" column on the worksheet to help you locate intervention resources. Notice that the prerequisite objectives and interventions are listed on the BIP in the order in which they will be addressed. The steps are summarized in the flowchart in Figure 2.3.

If you have questions or concerns related to the use of this program, please contact me for help. I can be reached c/o Department of Special and Counselor Education, Box 571, Portland State University, Portland, OR 97207, 503/725-4637, fax 503/725-5599, kaplanj@pdx.edu.

8. Responds Aggressively to Peer Provocation

AGG/PROV

Student ___Joey Johnson___   Evaluator ___Ms. Davis___   Date _____

MALADAPTIVE BEHAVIOR: Student responds to peer provocation (i.e., teasing, threats, swearing, insults, disapproval) with aggression (i.e., verbally and/or physically attacking peers).

Prerequisites	Status Y	N	?
1. Understands that when provoked by peers, he or she *is expected* to respond without any verbal or physical aggression.	☑	☐	☐
has paraphrased rule in past			
2. *Is aware* of when he or she is responding to peer provocation assertively and when he or she is responding aggressively.	☑	☐	☒
3. There are no factors (e.g., anger and/or impulsivity) currently *beyond the student's control* that would make it difficult for him or her to respond assertively, without any aggression, to peer provocation.	☐	☑	☒
4. *Has skills and knowledge* needed to respond to peer provocation assertively without aggression.	☑	☐	☒
5. *Considers consequences* of responding to peer provocation assertively and without aggression more rewarding (or less aversive) than responding with aggression.	☐	☑	☒
6. Does not hold any *beliefs incompatible* with responding to peer provocation assertively without aggression.	☐	☑	☒
7. *Perceives* assertive responding as a possible solution to the problem of peer provocation.	☑	☐	☒

Figure 2.1. Sample completed worksheet.

8. Responds Aggressively to Peer Provocation (*Continued*)

AGG/PROV

TARGET BEHAVIOR: When provoked by peers (i.e., teasing, threats, insulting, swearing, disapproval), the student responds assertively (i.e., tells peers to stop and what he or she feels about their behavior), without being aggressive.

Assessment (use only if status is ?)	Results	Intervention (use only if status is N)
ask student (see p. 63, #1)		direct instruction (see pp. 75, 110)
simultaneous estimation (see p. 63, #2)	Pass—his estimates w/in 10% of mine	self-monitoring (see pp. 76, 110–111)
peer comparison (see p. 63, #3)	No Pass—data resemble angry peer group	stress inoculation for anger (see pp. 76, 112) · self-instructional training for impulsivity (see pp. 76, 110)
role play test (see p. 64, #4)	Pass—meets CAP all 3 role plays	social skills training (see pp. 76, 111)
cue-sort exercise (see p. 64, #5)	No Pass—can't name all consequences of assertive behavior	verbal mediation (see pp. 76, 112) · behavior modification (see pp. 75, 109)
beliefs assessment (see p. 64, #6)	No Pass—answered items #3, 6, 13, 15, 20 true	cognitive restructuring (see pp. 75, 109–110)
generates solutions (see p. 65, #7)	Pass—generates several solutions including target behavior	problem solving (see pp. 76, 110)

Figure 2.1. *Continued.*

Behavior Intervention Plan

Student Joey Johnson   Planner(s) Ms. Davis/Mr. Marx   Date 5-9-00

Goal When provoked by peers, student responds assertively w/o aggression

Objective(s)	Intervention(s)	Responsible	Evaluation
1. When cued to do so, JJ will correctly name all consequences of assertive and aggressive responding to peer provocation w/o prompting w/in 20 seconds.	interest inventory begin 5-10-00	Mr. Marx	cue sort 1 wk. from begin date
2. Given all consequences of assertive and aggressive responses to peer provocation, JJ will identify all consequences of assertive responding as those he likes and all consequences of aggressive responding as those he dislikes.	verbal mediation daily as needed; begin after interest inventory completed	Mr. Marx	cue sort 1 wk. from begin date
3. Given a beliefs assessment, JJ will identify all beliefs compatible with assertive responding to peer provocation as true, and all beliefs incompatible with assertive responding as false. CAP: 2 consec. trials w/ 24-hr. latency.	cognitive restruct. in Counseling Office 30 minutes/3x per wk. begin 5-10-00	Ms. Davis	beliefs assess. 4 wks. from begin date
4. When teacher monitors frequency of obvious signs of anger in JJ and small peer sample, some with and some without signs of anger, over three separate trials, JJ's data more closely resemble data of peers w/o anger signs on 2/3 trials.	stress inoculation in SPED classroom 30 minutes/3x per wk. begin 5-24-00	Mr. Marx	peer comparison 4 wks. from begin date

Signed _____   Date _____

Signed _____   Date _____

Figure 2.2. Sample behavioral intervention plan based on findings of Beyond FA evaluation.

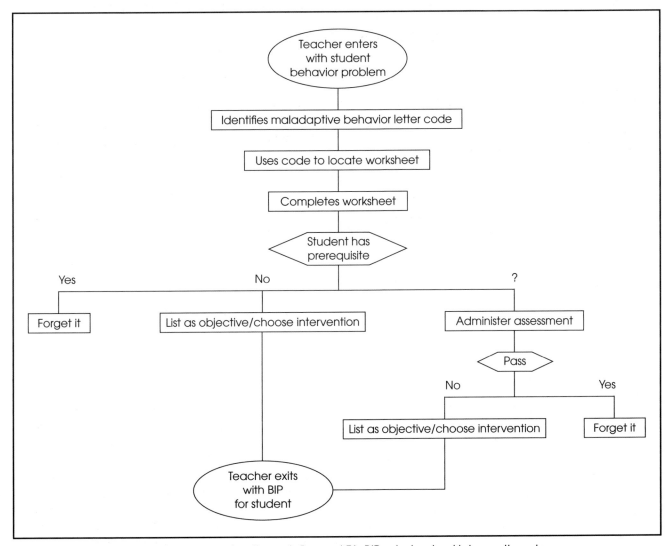

Figure 2.3. Flowchart outlining progression through Beyond FA. BIP = behavioral intervention plan.

Worksheets/Assessment Methods and Materials

1. Off Task Unless Supervised

WKS/SUP

Student _____ Evaluator _____ Date _____

MALADAPTIVE BEHAVIOR: Student does not work on assigned tasks unless supervised (i.e., adult standing over him or her providing verbal encouragement or threat of punishment).

Prerequisites	Status		
	Y	N	?
1. Understands he or she *is expected* to work on assigned tasks independently (i.e., with minimal or no supervision).	☐	☐	☐
2. *Is aware* of when he or she is and is not working on assigned tasks with and without supervision.	☐	☐	☐
3. There are no factors (e.g., depression, sensory impairment, medication or side effect of medication, distractibility associated with ADHD, seizure activity, communication disorder, or language barrier (i.e., English is student's second language)) currently *beyond the student's control* that make it difficult for him or her to work on assigned tasks without supervision.	☐	☐	☐
4. *Has skills and knowledge* needed to work on assigned tasks without supervision.	☐	☐	☐
5. *Considers consequences* of working on assigned tasks without supervision more rewarding (or less aversive) than not working on assigned tasks unless supervised.	☐	☐	☐
6. Does not hold any *beliefs incompatible* with working on assigned tasks without supervision.	☐	☐	☐

1. Off Task Unless Supervised (*Continued*)

WKS/SUP

TARGET BEHAVIOR: Student works on assigned tasks with minimal or no supervision.

Assessment (use only if status is ?)	Results	Intervention (use only if status is N)
ask student (see p. 30, #1)	_____ _____	direction instruction (see pp. 75, 110)
simultaneous monitoring (see p. 30, #2)	_____ _____	self-monitoring (see pp. 76, 110–111)
peer comparison (see pp. 30–31, #3)	_____ _____	stress inoculation for depression (see pp. 76, 110, 112)
medical history (see pp. 30–31, #3)	_____ _____	medical and/or environmental (see pp. 75–76)
curriculum-based assessment (see p. 31, #4)	_____ _____	remedial work (see pp. 76, 110)
cue-sort exercise (see pp. 31–32, #5)	_____ _____ _____	verbal mediation (see pp. 76, 112) behavior modification (see pp. 75, 109)
beliefs assessment (see p. 32, #6)	_____ _____	cognitive restructuring (see pp. 75, 109–110)

Assessments—WKS/SUP

1. Expectation

Ask Student: Read only boldface material to student. **"Tell me in your own words what you are supposed to do when I give you a task (work) to do in class."** The student's answer should convey the idea that he or she is expected to work on the task without prompting (reminders) from the teacher. If the student has difficulty supplying a correct response, switch to a select-response format (see p. 12 of this manual).

CAP: Answering correctly with little or no prompting within 10 seconds of being asked.

2. Self-Awareness

Simultaneous Monitoring: Give the student a task to work on at his or her desk and during that time, both you and the student simultaneously (but separately) monitor the frequency of his or her on- and off-task behavior using the following procedure:

(a) Apply one strip of masking tape around your wrist and one on the student's desk.

(b) Explain to the student what you want him or her to do. Say, **"Start working on the task on your desk. When you catch yourself looking away from the task on your desk** (model), **make a mark (/) on your desk tape** (model) **and go back to work** (model). **Now tell me what you are supposed to do and when you are supposed to do it."**

(c) Set a small kitchen timer to signal the end of the monitoring trial (as much time as you can afford to continuously watch the target student).

(d) Position yourself in the classroom where you can see the student but he or she cannot see you without being off task. Begin monitoring the student's off-task behavior in the manner described in (b) above. If you are the person in charge and you need to intervene to interrupt the student's off-task behavior, do so. If the student has not recorded his or her behavior on his or her tape, you may *remind him or her once*, but do not tell him or her what to mark. The student needs to remember to do it him- or herself.

(e) When the timer rings, stop monitoring the student's off-task behavior and remove the student's tape from his or her desk.

(f) Repeat steps (a) through (e) above for two more tasks (same day or next day).

(g) Calculate the percentage of agreement between your data and the student's data by adding up the total number of marks (/) on *all three trials* on your tapes and the total number of marks on *all three trials* on the student's tapes. Using the two totals, divide the larger total into the smaller total and multiply by 100 to get the percentage of interobserver agreement.

CAP: At least 80% interobserver agreement between your data and the student's data.

3. Self-Control

Peer Comparison: Use the observable signs of depression listed in Table 1.3 to help you select a small ($N = 2-4$) sample of peers, some with observable signs of depression and some without. Choose one or more of the observable signs from Table 1.3 to monitor both the target student and the peer sample. Because many observable signs of depression represent a decrease or absence of behavior, I suggest you monitor affect (facial expression) using the following procedure:

(a) Choose a time when the target student and the peer sample can be monitored at the same time, during an activity that is usually stimulating for your students (e.g., during free time or class discussion) and preferably when each is required to stay in one place in the room.

(b) Use a monitoring form like the one shown in Figure 3.1 *for each student.*

(c) As unobtrusively as possible, both *you and a second observer* (teaching partner, assistant, psychologist) look at each student, *one at a time (in the same order)* and record his or her level of affect *at the moment you look* at him or her. Use the key on the monitoring sheet to help you decide whether each student's affect is depressed (1), sad (2), interested (3), or happy (4), and record the corresponding number on the student's monitoring form.

(d) Observing, determining, and recording level of affect (i.e., 1, 2, 3, or 4) should take no more than 10 seconds per student. Use a watch with a beeper or a tape-recorded signal to tell you when to move from student to student. When you hear the signal, observe the first student and record his or her affect. When you hear the signal indicating the end of the 10-second interval, move on to the next student in the sequence and record his or her affect, and so on. When you finish with the last student in the sequence, start all over again. Make sure you and the second observer monitor the students in the same sequence (e.g.,

Student A, Student B, Student C, Student A, Student B, etc.). Do not look at each other's monitoring forms until you are finished collecting data.

(e) Continue to record in this manner until you have looked at the target student and the students in the peer sample *at least 12 times each. Important:* If, after 12 intervals, the data do not show a definitive difference between the target student and his or her peers, try increasing the number of intervals.

(f) You and the second observer calculate the percent of interobserver agreement between your sets of data by using the point-by-point agreement ratio (see p. 14 of this manual). There should be at least 80% agreement. If there is, proceed (see below). If not, refer to page 15 in this manual and try again.

(g) Assuming there is 80% agreement between you and the second observer, repeat steps (a) through (f) on two more monitoring trials (preferable over 2 or more days).

(h) Calculate the average level of affect (LOA) for each student *on each of the three trials.* Add all of the numbers in the boxes for one student and divide this sum by the total number of boxes with numbers in them (see Figure 3.1). Continue in this manner until you have three average LOAs per student. *Using the median LOA for each student,* compare the target student's data with the data of the peer sample.

CAP: *The target student's data (i.e., median LOA) more closely resemble data (i.e., median LOAs) of nondepressed* peers *than those of depressed peers.* See page 107 of this manual for additional depression assessments.

Medical History: Review the target student's medical history (see cumulative folder) and/or interview past teachers and others who know the target student to determine the presence of any of the following: sensory impairment (e.g., hearing or vision loss), use of medication, distractibility associated with ADHD, evidence of seizure activity (petit mal), communication disorder and/or language barrier (i.e., English not the student's first language).

CAP: *No evidence of any of the above conditions in student.*

4. Competence

Curriculum-Based Assessment: See pages 17 and 110 of this manual.

CAP: *The student is competent in all aspects of academic tasks assigned.*

5. Motivation

Cue Sort: You will need some blank 3 × 5 cards to write on. Read only boldface material to student.

(a) To see if the student knows the consequences of staying on task without supervision, ask him or her, **"What happens to you when you work on your assignments (tasks) on your own without being**

Student \ Interval 10"	1	2	3	4	5	6	7	8	9	10	11	12	LOA
J. J.	1	1	2	2	2	1	1	1	1	1	1	1	1.25
B. J.	3	4	4	3	3	3	4	3	3	4	3	3	3.3
L. O.	2	3	3	2	3	3	3	3	3	2	3	3	2.75

KEY: (1) depressed affect (no expression; staring into space; appears "out of it" or drugged)

(2) sad affect (some facial expression; eyes averted, oriented downward; mouth curved downward; appears sad)

(3) interested affect ("normal" facial expression; mouth curved upward or relaxed; eyes focused; appears interested in environment)

(4) happy affect (animated expression; smiling/laughing; eye movement)

Observer _____   Date _____

Figure 3.1. Monitoring level of affect (LOA) for depression.

reminded?" Write the student's responses on 3 × 5 cards, one response to a card.

(b) If the student has difficulty supplying the correct answers, switch to a select-response format (see p. 12 of this manual). If the student still has difficulty answering, tell him or her what the consequences are and write them down on the cards. Indicate on the back of each card whether the student supplied the consequence or you supplied it.

(c) To see if the student knows the consequences of being off task or working only if supervised, ask him or her, **"What happens to you when you don't do your work unless someone stands over you making sure that you do it?"** Write the student's responses on 3 × 5 cards, one response to a card. Follow the same procedure as above if the student has difficulty naming all of the consequences.

(d) When all of the consequences have been written down, mix them up by shuffling the deck of cards.

(e) Give the deck to the student and ask him or her to sort them according to likes and dislikes. Say, **"These are the things that happen to you in school when you work independently and when you need supervision to do your work. Please sort them into two groups—things you like and things you don't like. What are you supposed to do?"** Help the student get started by modeling what you want him or her to do. Help the student read some or all of the cards if necessary. If the student can't make up his or her mind about a consequence, put it in a third pile.

CAP: *All of the consequences for working independently should be identified as things the students likes and all of the consequences for working only when supervised should be identified as things the student dislikes.*

6. Beliefs

Beliefs Assessment: See pages 80–81 in Appendix A.

2. Excessive Movement in Classroom

INAPP/MOVE

Student _____ Evaluator _____ Date _____

MALADAPTIVE BEHAVIOR: Student engages in physical activity (i.e., movement) that is inappropriate according to frequency, situation, and setting in school (e.g., running in halls or classroom, out-of-seat without permission).

Prerequisites	Status Y	N	?
1. Understands he or she *is expected* to engage in physical activity in school that is appropriate according to frequency, situation, and setting.	☐	☐	☐
2. *Is aware* of when he or she is not engaging in physical activity in school that is appropriate according to frequency, situation, and setting.	☐	☐	☐
3. There are no factors (e.g., anxiety or impulsivity, hyperactivity associated with ADHD, medication) currently *beyond the student's control* that make it difficult for him or her to engage in physical activity at school that is appropriate according to frequency, situation, and setting.	☐	☐	☐
4. *Has skills and knowledge* needed to engage in physical activity at school that is appropriate according to frequency, situation, and setting.	☐	☐	☐
5. *Considers consequences* of engaging in physical activity at school that is appropriate according to frequency, situation, and setting to be more rewarding (or less aversive) than engaging in physical activity that is inappropriate.	☐	☐	☐
6. Does not hold any *beliefs incompatible* with engaging in physical activity at school that is appropriate according to frequency, situation, and setting.	☐	☐	☐

2. Excessive Movement in Classroom (*Continued*)

INAPP/MOVE

TARGET BEHAVIOR: Student engages in physical activity (movement) in school that is appropriate according to frequency, situation, and setting.

Assessment (use only if status is ?)	Results	Intervention (use only if status is N)
ask student (see p. 35, #1)	_____ _____	direct instruction (see pp. 75, 110)
simultaneous monitoring (see p. 35, #2)	_____ _____	self-monitoring (see pp. 76, 110–111)
peer comparison (see p. 35, #3)	_____ _____	stress inoculation for anxiety (see pp. 76, 110, 112) self-instructional training for impulsivity (see pp. 76, 110)
medical history (see p. 36, #3)	_____ _____	medical and/or environmental (see pp. 75–76)
role play test (see p. 36, #4)	_____ _____	social skills training (see pp. 76, 111)
cue-sort exercise (see p. 37, #5)	_____ _____ _____	verbal mediation (see pp. 76, 112) behavior modification (see pp. 75, 109)
beliefs assessment (see p. 37, #6)	_____ _____	cognitive restructuring (see pp. 75, 109–110)

Assessments—INAPP≠MOVE

1. Expectation

Ask Student: Read only boldface material to student. **"Tell me in your own words how you are supposed to use your body (run, walk, sit, stand) in the (classroom, halls, playground, cafeteria, gym) when it is (free time, independent seatwork, class lesson, moving between classrooms, lunch recess, assemblies)."** The student's answers should convey the idea that he or she is expected to sit and to walk in all settings and situations except for the playground and gym. If the student has difficulty supplying a correct response, switch to a select-response format (see p. 12 of this manual).

CAP: Answering correctly with little or no prompting within 10 seconds of being asked.

2. Awareness

Simultaneous Monitoring: You and the student each monitor the frequency of his or her inappropriate movement *in the classroom* using the following procedure:

(a) Choose an interval of time in the classroom when it is feasible for both you and the target student to monitor his or her movement.

(b) Apply one strip of masking tape around your wrist and one around the target student's wrist. Explain to the student what you want him or her to do. Say, **"During the next** (you decide) **minutes, I want you to keep track of how many times you are out of your seat, away from your seat, or running in the room** (model each for student). **Each time you find yourself doing any of these three behaviors, make a mark like this (/) on your wrist tape** (model). **Here is a marker. Keep it in your pocket. Now tell me what you are supposed to do."**

(c) Set a small kitchen timer to signal the end of the monitoring trial (for as much time as you can continuously watch student).

(d) Sit in a place in the classroom where you can see the student but where he or she will not be able to see you record your data. Cue the student to begin his or her self-monitoring as you start your monitoring.

(e) If someone in charge needs to intervene to interrupt the student's inappropriate movement, he or she should do so. If the student has not recorded his or her behavior on his or her tape, you may remind the student once but do not tell him or her what to

mark. The student needs to remember to do it him- or herself.

(f) When the timer rings, signaling the end of the monitoring interval, cue the student to stop and remove the tape from his or her wrist.

(g) Repeat steps (a) through (e) above for two additional trials (same day or next day).

(h) Calculate the percentage of agreement between your data and the student's data by adding up the total number of marks (/) on *all three trials* on your tapes and the total number of marks on *all three trials* on the student's tapes. Using the two totals, divide the larger total into the smaller total and multiply by 100 to get the percentage of interobserver agreement.

CAP: At least 80% interobserver agreement between your data and the student's data.

3. Self-Control

Peer Comparison: Use the observable signs of anxiety in Table 1.3 to help you select a small (N = 2–4) sample of students, some with observable signs of anxiety and some without. Choose one or more of the anxiety signs listed in the table to monitor both the target student and the peer sample using the following procedure:

(a) Choose a time when the target student and the peer sample can be monitored at the same time, during an activity that might elicit anxiety in the students (e.g., social interactions or academics) and preferably when they (with the possible exception of the target student) are likely to stay in one place.

(b) Use a monitoring form similar to example shown in Figure 3.2 for each student.

(c) As unobtrusively as possible, both *you and a second observer* (teaching partner, assistant, psychologist) observe each student *one at a time and in the same order* for a 10-second interval (either count to yourself or set the timer on your watch). If the student you are watching engages in one or more of the anxiety signs you are monitoring *at any time during that interval,* record a mark (/) in a box next to the student's name. Then move on to the next student, observe and record for 10 seconds, move on to the next student, and so on. Make sure that you and the second observer do not look at each other's monitoring forms. When you finish with the last student, start all over again.

| Observer _____ Date _____ |
| Counted *verbalizations* (e.g., "This is scary") and *movement* (e.g., rocking, pacing) |

Interval 10" / Student	1	2	3	4	5	6	7	8	9	10	11	12	F
M. B.	1	1	1	1	1	1	0	1	1	0	1	0	9
J. R.	0	1	1	1	0	0	1	0	0	0	0	0	4
L. O.	0	0	0	1	1	0	0	0	0	0	0	0	2
J. K.	0	0	0	0	1	1	0	0	0	0	0	0	2

Figure 3.2. Monitoring frequency of anxiety displays (use also for anger, impulsivity with different behavioral correlates).

(d) Continue to observe and record in this manner until you have *at least 12 intervals* completed for each student.

(e) You and the second observer calculate the percentage of interobserver agreement between your sets of data by finding the total number of anxiety signs (/) each of you recorded and dividing the larger total into the smaller total. There should be at least 80% agreement. If there is, proceed (see below). If not, refer to page 15 in this manual and try again.

(f) Assuming there is 80% agreement between you and the second observer, repeat steps (a) through (e) on two more monitoring trials preferably over 2 or more days.

(g) Find the median for each student's *three trial scores* and compare the target student's median with the median scores for each of the students in the peer sample.

CAP: *The target student's data (i.e., median score) more closely resemble data (i.e., median scores) of nonanxious peers than the anxious peers. See page 107 of this manual for additional anxiety assessments.*

Use the same procedure and the same type of monitoring form to monitor the frequency of impulsivity in the target student and a small sample of peers, some with impulse control and some without. Use Table 1.3 to help you select the peer sample and the observable signs of impulsivity to monitor.

CAP: *The target student's data (i.e., median score) more closely resemble data (i.e., median scores) of the nonimpulsive*

peers *than the data of the impulsive peers. See page 108 of this* manual for additional impulsivity assessments.

Medical History: Review the target student's medical history and/or interview past teachers and other individuals with knowledge of the student to determine the presence of ADHD and/or use of stimulant medication.

CAP: *No evidence of ADHD or use of stimulant medications.*

4. Competence

Role Play Test: You may change any or all of the role play situations below if they are not age appropriate for your student(s), the vocabulary is too difficult, or the situations are unrealistic. In each case write down what the student says and/or does.

(a) Read only boldface material to the student. Say, **"I want you to role-play (act out) each of the things I ask you to do. Don't tell me, *show me.***"

(b) **"Show me how you can stay in your seat during a classroom lesson."** (Play an audiotape of a teacher giving a lesson to the class so that the target student hears the teacher and the background noise of the class).

CAP: *Student should stay in seat—buttocks touching chair and both feet on floor under desk—for a time period to be determined as acceptable by teacher.*

(c) **"Now I want you to go from your desk to different places in the room. Show me how you can do** this quickly and carefully, without running or bumping into furniture. Ready? Here is a pencil. Go to the pencil sharpener, sharpen it, and go back to your desk. (pause) Go to the blackboard and write your name on it with some chalk. Then go back to your desk." (pause)

CAP: Student can move about the classroom, walking without running or bumping into furniture.

(d) **"Go to my desk and get the hall pass, leave the room, and go to the office. I will follow you. (pause) Now return to the classroom."**

CAP: Student can move from classroom to office without running.

CAP (overall): The student (in your judgment) meets each of the individual CAPs for the aforementioned physical activities.

5. Motivation

Cue Sort: You will need some blank 3 × 5 cards to write on. Read only boldface material to the student.

(a) To see if the student knows the consequences of engaging in physical activity that is appropriate according to frequency, situation, and setting in the school, ask him or her, **"What happens to you when you walk and don't run in the hallway, classroom, cafeteria, and you stay in your seat when you are supposed to** (add or substitute any other examples of appropriate physical activity required of students in your school)?" Write the student's responses on 3 × 5 cards, one response to a card.

(b) If the student has difficulty supplying a correct response, switch to a select-response format (see p. 12 of this manual). Write the student's responses on 3 × 5 cards, one response to a card. Indicate on the back of each card if the student supplied the consequence or you supplied it.

(c) If the student continues to have difficulty, tell him or her what the responses are and write them down on the cards.

(d) To see if the student knows the consequences of engaging in inappropriate physical activity in the classroom, ask him or her, **"What happens to you when you are out of your seat without permission, run in the classroom, jump up out of your seat, or run in the hall** (add or substitute any other inappropriate physical activity the student engages in)?" Write the student's responses on 3 × 5 cards, one response to a card.

(e) Follow the same procedure as above (c) if the student doesn't name all of the negative consequences.

(f) When all of the consequences have been written down, mix them up by shuffling the cards.

(g) Give the cards to the student and ask him or her to sort them according to likes and dislikes. Say, **"Here are some things that happen to you in school when you (stay in your seat, walk in the classroom) and when you (are out of your seat and run in the room and in the halls). Sort them into two groups—things you like and things you dislike."** Help the student get started by modeling what you want him or her to do. Help the student read some or all of the cards if necessary. If he or she can't make up his or her mind about a consequence, put it in a third pile.

CAP: All of the consequences for appropriate physical activity in the school should be identified as things the student likes and all of the consequences for inappropriate physical activity in the school should be identified as things the student dislikes.

6. Beliefs

Beliefs Assessment: See pages 82–83 in Appendix A.

3. Noncompliant

NONCOMP

Student _____ Evaluator _____ Date _____

MALADAPTIVE BEHAVIOR: Given directives that all students are expected to follow at school, the student does not follow at all, is slow to follow, or performs in an unacceptable fashion.

Prerequisites	Status		
	Y	N	?
1. Understands that when given a directive expected of all students at school, he or she *is expected* to follow it the first time given and in an acceptable fashion.	☐	☐	☐
2. *Is aware* of when he or she is and is not following directives the first time given and in an acceptable fashion.	☐	☐	☐
3. There are no factors (e.g., anxiety, depression, hearing loss, language barrier) currently *beyond the student's control* that make it difficult for him or her to follow directives the first time given and in an acceptable fashion.	☐	☐	☐
4. Has *skills and knowledge* needed to successfully follow directives at school.	☐	☐	☐
5. *Considers consequences* of following directives the first time given and in an acceptable fashion more rewarding (or less aversive) than not following directives.	☐	☐	☐
6. Does not hold any *beliefs incompatible* with following directives the first time given and in an acceptable fashion.	☐	☐	☐

3. Noncompliant (*Continued*)

TARGET BEHAVIOR: Given directives that all students are expected to follow at school, the student follows them the first time given and in an acceptable fashion (i.e., acceptable according to teacher or school standards).

Assessment (use only if status is ?)	Results	Intervention (use only if status is N)
ask student (see p. 40, #1)	_____ _____	direct instruction (see pp. 75, 110)
simultaneous monitoring (see p. 40, #2)	_____ _____	self-monitoring (see pp. 76, 110–111)
peer comparison (see p. 40, #3)	_____ _____	stress inoculation for anger (see pp. 76, 110, 112)
medical history and/or speech pathology (see p. 41, #3)	_____ _____	medical and/or environmental (see pp. 75–76)
curriculum-based assessment (see p. 41, #4)	_____ _____	remedial work (see pp. 76, 110)
cue-sort exercise (see p. 41, #5)	_____ _____ _____ _____	verbal mediation (see pp. 76, 112) / behavior modification (see pp. 75, 109)
beliefs assessment (see p. 41, #6)	_____ _____	cognitive restructuring (see pp. 75, 109–110)

Assessments—NONCOMP

Important: If, at any time, the target student refuses to cooperate in the assessment process, your options are to stop for the moment and try again later or to assume that the student is lacking that prerequisite and go on to the next one.

1. Expectation

Ask Student: Read only boldface material to student. **"Tell me in your own words what you are supposed to do when a teacher (staff member, administrator) at school asks you to do something."** The student's answer should convey the idea that as long as the behavior is expected of all students, he or she is expected to comply the first time asked and in a fashion deemed acceptable by the adult making the request. If the student has difficulty supplying a correct response, switch to a select-response format (see p. 12 of this manual).

CAP: Answering correctly with little or no prompting within 10 seconds of being asked.

2. Awareness

Simultaneous Monitoring: You and the student simultaneously (but separately) monitor the frequency of his or her compliant and noncompliant behavior using the following procedure:

(a) Estimate the minimum number of directives the student is given over a fixed amount of time (e.g., 30 to 60 minutes). Draw *at least* this number of boxes on each of two strips of masking tape. Apply one strip around your wrist and one around the student's wrist.

(b) Explain to the student what you want him or her to do. Say, **"For the next** (you decide how long) **minutes, I want you to keep track of the times you do and don't do as you are asked. Each time an adult in this class asks you to do something that is expected of all students and you do it the way you are supposed to without being asked more than once, make a + in one of the boxes on your wrist tape.** (Model for the student.) **Each time the adult has to repeat his or her request because you didn't do it right the first time or you didn't do it at all, make a 0 in one of the boxes on your wrist tape.** (Model.) **Keep doing this until the time is up and I ask you for the tape. Now tell me what you are supposed to do."**

(c) Set a timer (or your watch) to signal the end of the monitoring trial and cue the student when the monitoring begins.

(d) Position yourself in the room so that you can observe the student but he or she cannot observe you, and begin monitoring in the manner described above.

(e) If the student does not record his or her behavior on his or her tape when he or she should, you may *remind the student once* but do not tell him or her what to record in the box. The student needs to decide that him- or herself.

(f) Continue until the timer rings, signaling the end of the monitoring trial. Cue the student to stop monitoring and remove his or her wrist tape.

(g) Repeat steps (a) through (f) for two additional trials (may be same day or next).

(h) Calculate the percentage of agreement between your data and the target student's data by adding up the total number of 0's *on all three* of your tapes and the total number of 0's *on all three* of the student's tapes. Divide the larger total into the smaller total and multiply by 100.

CAP: At least 80% interobserver agreement between the teacher's data and the student's data.

3. Self-Control

Peer Comparison: Use Table 1.3 to help you select a small (*N* = 2–4) sample of students, some with observable signs of anxiety and some without. Choose one or more of the anxiety signs listed in the table to monitor, and use the following procedure:

(a) Choose a time for monitoring when the target student and the peer sample can be monitored at the same time, during an activity that typically elicits anxiety in the students (e.g., social interactions or academics) and, preferably, when they can each stay in one place.

(b) Use a monitoring form similar to the example shown in Figure 3.2.

(c) As unobtrusively as possible, both *you and a second observer* (teaching partner, assistant, psychologist) observe each student *one at a time in and the same order* for a 10-second interval (either count to yourself or set the timer on your watch). If the student you are watching engages in one or more of the anxiety signs you are monitoring *at any time during that interval,* record a mark (/) in a box next to the student's name. Then move on to the next student, observe and record for 10 seconds, move on to the next student, and so on. Make sure that you and the second observer do not look at each other's monitoring forms. When you finish with the last student, start all over again.

(d) Continue to observe and record in this manner until you have at least 12 intervals completed for each student.

(e) Compute the percentage of interobserver agreement between your data and that of the second observer by finding the total number of anxiety signs (/) each of you recorded and dividing the larger total into the smaller total. Assuming there is at least 80% agreement between you and the second observer on the first monitoring trial, repeat steps (a) through (e) for two more trials, preferably over 2 different days. If the percentage of agreement is less than 80%, refer to page 15 before proceeding.

(f) Find the median for each student's three trial scores and compare the target student's median with the median scores for each of the students in the peer sample.

CAP: The target student's data (i.e., median scores) more closely resemble data (i.e., median scores) of nonanxious peers than the data of the anxious peers. (See page 107 of this manual for additional anxiety assessments.)

Medical History: Review the target student's medical history and/or interview past teachers and other individuals with knowledge of the student to determine the presence of a hearing loss, communication disorder, or language barrier (i.e., English is student's second language).

CAP: No evidence of any of the above conditions in the student.

4. Competence

Curriculum-Based Assessment: See pages 17 and 110.

CAP: The student is competent at performing all of the directives given.

5. Motivation

Cue Sort: You will need some blank 3 × 5 cards to write on. Read only boldface material to student.

(a) To see if the student knows the consequences of compliance with directives, ask him or her, **"What happens to you when an adult here at school asks you to do something that is expected of all students and you comply (do it)?"** Write the student's responses on 3 × 5 cards, one consequence to a card.

(b) If the student has difficulty supplying the consequences of compliance, switch to a select-response format (see p. 12 of this manual). If he or she continues to have difficulty, tell him or her the consequences and write them down on the cards. Indicate on the back of each card whether the student named the consequence or you did.

(c) Repeat the above procedure for the consequences of noncompliance. Ask the student, **"What happens to you when an adult here at school asks you to do something that is expected of all students and you *do not* comply (*refuse* to do it) or you don't do it the way you are expected to?** Write the student's responses on 3 × 5 cards. Follow the same procedure as (b) if the student doesn't name all of the consequences of noncompliance.

(d) When all of the consequences have been written down, mix the cards up by shuffling the deck.

(e) Give the deck of cards to the student and ask him or her to sort them according to likes and dislikes. Say, **"Here are some things that happen to you in school when you follow directives and when you don't follow directives. Sort them into two groups—things you like and things you dislike."** Help the student get started by modeling what you want him or her to do. Help the student read the cards if necessary. If he or she can't make up his or her mind about a consequence, have him or her put the card in a third pile.

CAP: All of the consequences for compliance should be identified as things the student likes and all of the consequences for inappropriate responding to refusals should be identified as things the student dislikes.

6. Beliefs

Beliefs Assessment: See pages 84–85 in Appendix A.

4. Disruptive Attention Seeking

DIS/ATT SEEK

Student _____   Evaluator _____   Date _____

MALADAPTIVE BEHAVIOR: When seeking attention from peers or adults during academic instruction time, student engages in disruptive behavior (e.g., calling out, making noise, talking loudly, moving excessively).

Prerequisites	Status		
	Y	N	?
1. Understands that when seeking attention during academic instruction time, he or she *is expected* to do so in ways that do not disrupt the learning environment (e.g., raising his or her hand and waiting to be called on, speaking quietly, making eye contact).	☐	☐	☐
2. *Is aware* of when he or she is seeking attention in disruptive and non-disruptive ways.	☐	☐	☐
3. There are no factors (e.g., impulsivity, anxiety, or hyperactivity associated with ADHD) currently *beyond the student's control* that would make it difficult for him or her to seek attention in nondisruptive ways.	☐	☐	☐
4. *Has skills and knowledge* needed to seek attention in nondisruptive ways.	☐	☐	☐
5. *Considers consequences* of seeking attention in nondisruptive ways more rewarding (or less aversive) than acting in disruptive ways.	☐	☐	☐
6. Does not hold any *beliefs incompatible* with seeking attention in non-disruptive ways.	☐	☐	☐

4. Disruptive Attention Seeking (*Continued*)

TARGET BEHAVIOR: When seeking attention from peers or adults during academic instruction time, student does so in a nondisruptive manner (e.g., raises hand and waits, speaks quietly, makes eye contact).

Assessment (use only if status is ?)	Results	Intervention (use only if status is N)
ask student (see p. 44, #1)	_____ _____	direct instruction (see pp. 75, 110)
simultaneous monitoring (see p. 44, #2)	_____ _____	self-monitoring (see pp. 76, 110–111)
peer comparison (see p. 44, #3)	_____ _____	stress inoculation for anxiety (see pp. 76, 112)
	_____	self-instructional training for impulsivity (see pp. 76, 110)
medical history (see p. 45, #3)	_____ _____	medical and/or environmental (see pp. 75–76)
role play test (see p. 45, #4)	_____ _____	social skills (see pp. 76, 111)
cue-sort exercise (see p. 45, #5)	_____ _____	verbal mediation (see pp. 76, 112)
	_____ _____	behavior modification (see pp. 75, 109)
beliefs assessment (see p. 46, #6)	_____ _____	cognitive restructuring (see pp. 75, 109–110)

Assessments—DIS/ATT SEEK

1. Expectation

Ask Student: Read only boldface material to the student. **"Tell me in your own words what you are supposed to do when you want someone's attention in the classroom."** The student's answer should convey the idea that he or she is supposed to use nondisruptive means (e.g., raise hand and wait, speak quietly, make eye contact, stay in one place). If the student has difficulty supplying a correct response, switch to a select-response format (see p. 12 of this manual).

CAP: Answering correctly with little or no prompting within 10 seconds of being asked.

2. Awareness

Simultaneous Monitoring: Both you and the student simultaneously (but separately) monitor the frequency of his or her disruptive and nondisruptive attention-seeking behavior using the following procedure:

(a) Apply a strip of masking tape around your wrist and another strip around the target student's wrist (or on his or her desk top).

(b) Explain to the student what you want him or her to do. Say, **"For the next** (you decide how long) **minutes, I want you to keep track of the times you shout out in class to get my attention (or someone else's attention)** (model)**. Each time this happens, I want you to make a mark (/) on your tape** (model)**. Now tell me what you are supposed to do and when you are supposed to do it."**

(c) Set a timer (or your watch) to signal the end of the monitoring trial (for as much time as you can afford to continuously watch the target student). Cue the target student when the monitoring begins.

(d) Position yourself in the room where you can see the student but he or she cannot observe you, and begin monitoring in the manner described above.

(e) If at any time during the monitoring interval the student's attention-seeking behavior becomes intolerable (i.e., makes it impossible to teach and/or has potential for aggression), whoever is in charge should intervene.

(f) The student who is not properly recording his or her behavior may be reminded once.

(g) When the timer rings, stop your monitoring, cue the student to stop monitoring, and remove the tape from his or her wrist or desk.

(h) Repeat steps (a) through (g) for two additional trials (either same day or next day).

(i) Calculate the percentage of agreement between your data and the student's data by adding up the total number of marks (/) on *all three trials* on your tapes and the total number of marks on *all three trials* on the student's tapes. Using the two totals, divide the larger total into the smaller total and multiply by 100 to get the percentage of interobserver agreement.

CAP: At least 80% interobserver agreement between your data and the student's data.

3. Self-Control

Peer Comparison: Use Table 1.3 to help you select a small ($N = 2-4$) sample of students, some with observable signs of anxiety and some without. Choose one or more of the anxiety signs listed in the table to monitor, and use the following procedure:

(a) Choose a time when the target student and the peer sample can be monitored simultaneously, during an activity that might elicit anxiety in the students (e.g., free time or class discussion) and preferably when they are required to stay in one place in the room.

(b) Use a monitoring form similar to the example in Figure 3.2.

(c) As unobtrusively as possible, both you *and a second observer* (teaching partner, assistant, psychologist) glance at each student *one at a time (in the same order)* for a 10-second interval (either count to yourself or set the timer on your watch). If the student you are watching engages in one or more of the anxiety signs you are monitoring during that interval, record a mark (/) on the form.

(d) Continue to observe and record in this manner until you have *at least 12 intervals* completed for each student.

(e) Compute the percentage of interobserver agreement between your data and that of the second observer by finding the total number of anxiety signs (/) each of you recorded and dividing the larger total into the smaller total. Assuming there is at least 80% agreement between you and the second observer on the first monitoring trial, repeat steps

(a) through (e) for two more trials, preferably over 2 different days. If the percentage of agreement is less than 80%, refer to page 15 of this manual before proceeding.

(f) Find the median for each student's three trial scores and compare the target student's median with the median scores for each of the students in the peer sample.

CAP: The target student's data (i.e., median score) more closely resemble data (i.e., median scores) of nonanxious peers than data of the anxious peers. See page 107 of this manual for additional anxiety assessments.

Use the same procedure and the same type of monitoring form you used to monitor anxiety to monitor the frequency of impulsivity in the target student and a small sample of peers, some with impulse control and some without. Use Table 1.3 to help select the peer monitoring sample.

CAP: The target student's data more closely resemble data of the nonimpulsive peers than the data of the impulsive peers. See page 108 for additional assessments for impulsivity.

Medical History: Review the target student's medical history and/or interview past teachers and others with knowledge of the student to determine the presence of hyperactivity associated with ADHD.

CAP: No evidence of hyperactivity associated with ADHD.

4. Competence

Role Play Test: You may change any or all of the role play situations below if they are not age appropriate for your student(s), the vocabulary is too difficult, or the situations are unrealistic. In each case, write down what the student says and/or does.

(a) Read only boldface material to student. Say, **"I want you to role-play (act out) with me how you would try to get my attention in each of the following situations. Don't tell me what you would do; *show me*."**

(b) Have the target student sit at his or her desk while you stand with your back to him or her at another student's desk. Say, **"I am working with another student at her desk. You want to use the hall pass but you can't leave your seat without permission. Show me how you would get my attention without disrupting the class."**

(c) Have the target student sit at his or her desk while you stand in the front of the room talking to the class. Say, **"Everyone in the class is supposed to be working quietly at their desks. You want to ask (student) sitting across the room from you a question. Show me how you would do this without disrupting the class."**

(d) **"You want to answer a question I have asked the class. Show me how you would get my attention to answer the question without disrupting the class."**

CAP: The student (in your judgment) is able to demonstrate (i.e., role-play) appropriate attention-seeking behavior in at least two of the three situations without any prompting from you. "Appropriate" attention-seeking behavior includes any combination of raising one's hand and waiting, speaking quietly, making eye contact, and staying in one's place.

5. Motivation

Cue Sort: You will need some blank 3 × 5 cards. Read only boldface material to student.

(a) To see if the student knows the consequences of seeking attention from peers and adults in a nondisruptive manner, ask him or her, **"What happens to you when you try to get someone's attention in the classroom in a quiet way that doesn't disturb others?"** Write the student's responses on 3 × 5 cards, one response to a card.

(b) If the student has difficulty supplying the correct answers, switch to a select-response format (see p. 12 of this manual). Write the student's responses on 3 × 5 cards, one response to a card. Indicate on the back of each card whether the student supplied the consequence or you supplied it.

(c) If the student continues to have difficulty, tell him or her what the consequences are and write them down on the cards.

(d) To see if the student knows the consequences of disruptive attention seeking, ask him or her, **"What happens to you when you try to get someone's attention in the classroom in a way that disturbs others?"** Write these down on the cards and follow the above procedure if the student doesn't name all of the negative consequences.

(e) When all of the consequences have been written down, shuffle the cards.

(f) Give the cards to the student and ask him or her to sort them according to likes and dislikes. Say, **"Here are some things that happen to you in school. Sort**

them into two groups—things you like and things you dislike." Help the student get started by modeling what you want him or her to do. Help him or her read the cards if necessary. If he or she can't make up his or her mind about a consequence, put it in a third pile.

CAP: *All of the consequences for seeking attention without being disruptive should be identified as things the student likes* *and all of the consequences for seeking attention by being disruptive should be identified as things the student dislikes.*

6. Beliefs

Beliefs Assessment: See pages 86–87 in Appendix A.

5. Tantrums When Requests Refused   TANT/REFUS

Student _____ Evaluator _____ Date _____

MALADAPTIVE BEHAVIOR: When student's requests are not met by a peer or an adult at school, he or she engages in tantrum behavior (e.g., crying, shouting, cursing, destroying or throwing objects, etc.).

Prerequisites	Status Y	N	?
1. Understands that when his or her requests are not met, he or she *is expected* to respond in a prosocial way (i.e., repeat request, ask for an explanation, try to negotiate, and/or accept the refusal).	☐	☐	☐
2. *Is aware* of when he or she is responding to refusals in a prosocial and anti-social manner (i.e., throwing tantrum).	☐	☐	☐
3. There are no factors (e.g., anger) currently *beyond the student's control* that would make it difficult for him or her to respond to refusals in a prosocial manner.	☐	☐	☐
4. *Has skills and knowledge* needed to respond to refusals in a prosocial manner.	☐	☐	☐
5. *Considers consequences* of responding to refusals in a prosocial manner more rewarding (or less aversive) than responding in an antisocial manner.	☐	☐	☐
6. Does not hold any *beliefs incompatible* with responding to refusals in prosocial manner.	☐	☐	☐
7. Perceives repeating request, asking "Why not?," negotiating, and accepting decision as possible *solutions to problem* of having request refused.	☐	☐	☐

5. Tantrums When Requests Refused *(Continued)*

TARGET BEHAVIOR: When student's requests are not met by a peer or member of school staff, he or she will respond in a prosocial manner (e.g., repeat request, ask for explanation, negotiate, and/or accept refusal).

Assessment (use only if status is ?)	Results	Intervention (use only if status is N)
ask student (see p. 49, #1)	_____ _____	direct instruction (see pp. 75, 110)
simultaneous monitoring (see p. 49, #2)	_____ _____	self-monitoring (see pp. 76, 110–111)
peer comparison (see p. 49, #3)	_____ _____	stress inoculation for anger (see pp. 76, 112)
role play test (see p. 50, #4)	_____ _____	social skills training (see pp. 76, 111)
cue-sort exercise (see p. 50, #5)	_____ _____ _____ _____	verbal mediation (see pp. 76, 112) behavior modification (see pp. 75, 109)
beliefs assessment (see p. 51, #6)	_____ _____	cognitive restructuring (see pp. 75, 109–110)
generates solutions (see p. 51, #7)	_____ _____	problem solving (see pp. 76, 110)

Assessments—TANT/REFUS

1. Expectation

Ask Student: Read only boldface material to student. **"Tell me in your own words what you are supposed to do when someone does not do what you want him or her to do."** The student's answer should convey the idea that he or she is expected to respond in a prosocial manner (e.g., repeat the request, ask for explanation, negotiate, and/or accept refusal). If the student has difficulty supplying a correct response, switch to a select-response format (see p. 12 of this manual).

CAP: Answering correctly with little or no prompting within 10 seconds of being asked.

2. Awareness

Simultaneous Monitoring: You and the student simultaneously (but separately) monitor the frequency of his or her prosocial and antisocial responses to refusals at school using the following procedure:

(a) Identify an interval of time during the school day when you have the opportunity to observe the target student and his or her peers.

(b) Estimate the approximate number of requests made by the target student of adults and/or his or her peers during this interval of time. Draw this number of boxes on each of two strips of masking tape. Each box represents a request made by the student that is refused by the other person. The student's response to that refusal is recorded inside each box. Apply one strip around your wrist and the other around the target student's wrist.

(c) Explain to the student what you want him or her to do. Say, **"For the next** (you decide how long) **minutes, I want you to keep track of what you do when someone refuses to do what you want him or her to do. If you repeat the request, ask for an explanation, try to negotiate, or accept the refusal without getting upset, I want you to mark a + inside one of the boxes on your wrist tape.** (Model for the student.) **If you cry, shout, curse, or destroy or throw things, mark a 0 inside one of the boxes. Now tell me what you are supposed to do."**

(d) Set a timer (or your watch) to signal the end of the monitoring trial and cue the target student to begin monitoring.

(e) Position yourself in the room so that you can observe the student but he or she cannot observe you, and begin monitoring in the manner described above.

(f) If the student does not record his or her behavior on his or her tape when he or she should, you may *remind the student once,* but do not tell him or her what to record in the box. The student needs to decide that him- or herself.

(g) Continue until the timer signals the end of the monitoring trial. Cue the student to stop monitoring and remove his or her wrist tape.

(h) Repeat steps (a) through (g) for two additional trials (may be same day or next).

(i) Calculate the percentage of agreement between your data and the target student's data by adding up the total number of 0's *on all three* of your tapes and the total number of 0's *on all three* of the student's tapes. Divide the larger total into the smaller total and multiply by 100.

CAP: At least 80% interobserver agreement between the teacher's data and the student's data.

3. Self-Control

Peer Comparison: Use Table 1.3 to help select a small (*N* = 2–3) sample of students, some with observable signs of anger and some without. Choose one or more of the anger signs listed in the table to monitor, and use the following procedure:

(a) Choose a time for monitoring when the target student and the peer sample can be monitored simultaneously, during an activity that typically elicits anger in the students, preferably when they are not moving around (e.g., class discussion or lesson).

(b) Use a monitoring form similar to the example in Figure 3.2.

(c) As unobtrusively as possible, both you *and a second observer* (teaching partner, assistant, psychologist) glance at each student *one at a time (in the same order)* for a 10-second interval (either count to yourself or set the timer on your watch). If the student you are watching engages in one or more of the anger signs you are monitoring *at any time during that interval,* record a mark (/) in a box next to the student's name. Then move on to the next student, observe and record for 10 seconds, move on to the next student, and so on. Make sure that you and the second observer do not look at each other's monitoring forms. When you finish with the last student, start all over again.

(d) Continue to observe and record in this manner until you have at least 12 intervals completed for each student.

(e) Compute the percentage of interobserver agreement between your data and those of the second observer by finding the total number of anger signs (/) each of you recorded and dividing the larger total into the smaller total. Assuming there is at least 80% agreement between you and the second observer on the first monitoring trial, repeat steps (a) through (e) for two more trials, preferably over 2 different days. If the percentage of agreement is less than 80%, refer to page 15 of this manual before proceeding.

(f) Find the median for each student's three trial scores and compare the target student's median with the median scores for each of the students in the peer sample.

CAP: The target student's data (i.e., median scores) more closely resemble data (i.e., median scores) of nonangry peers than those of the angry peers. See page 107 of this manual for additional anger assessments.

4. Competence

Role Play Test: You may change any or all of the role play situations below if they are not age appropriate for your student(s) or the vocabulary is too difficult.

(a) Read only boldface material to student. Say, **"I want you to role-play (act out) with me how you should behave when someone refuses to do what you want them to do. Don't tell me what you would do; *show me*."** In each case, write down what the student says and/or does.

(b) **"You ask me if you can leave the room to go to your locker and I say 'no.' Show me how you would respond in an acceptable way."**

(c) **"I ask for a volunteer to pass out the test papers. You raise your hand but I call on someone else. Show me how you would respond in an acceptable way."**

(d) **"We are going out to recess and you want to carry out the jump ropes, but I choose someone else to do it. Show me how you would respond in an acceptable way."**

CAP: The student (in your judgment) is able to demonstrate (i.e., role-play) a socially appropriate response in at least two of the three situations without any prompting from you. A "socially appropriate response" requires that he or she does one or more of the following: repeats request (no more than twice after first refusal), asks for an explanation (once), tries to negotiate (i.e., seeks a compromise), or accepts refusal without incident.

5. Motivation

Cue Sort: You will need some blank 3 × 5 cards to write on. Read only boldface material to the student.

(a) To see if the student knows the consequences of prosocial responding to refusals, ask him or her, **"What happens to you when you ask for something and the person refuses and you repeat your request (ask for explanation, try to negotiate, accept refusal) without getting upset?"** Write the student's responses on 3 × 5 cards, one response to a card.

(b) If the student has difficulty supplying the correct answers, switch to a select-response format (see p. 12 of this manual). Write the student's responses on 3 × 5 cards, one response to a card. Indicate on the back of each card whether the student supplied the consequence or you supplied it.

(c) If the student continues to have difficulty, tell him or her what the consequences are and write them down on the cards.

(d) To see if the student knows the consequences of antisocial responding to refusals, ask him or her, **"What happens to you when you ask for something and the person refuses and you get upset and cry (shout, curse, or destroy or throw objects)?"** Write the student's responses on 3 × 5 cards, one response to a card.

(e) Follow the same procedure as above if the student doesn't name all of the negative consequences.

(f) When all of the consequences have been written down, shuffle the cards.

(g) Give the cards to the student and ask him or her to sort them according to likes and dislikes. Say, **"Here are some things that happen to you in school when you respond to refusals in an acceptable way and in an unacceptable way. Sort them into two groups—things you like and things you dislike."** Help the student get started by modeling what you want him or her to do. Help the student read the cards if necessary. If he or she can't make up his or her mind about a consequence, put it in a third pile.

CAP: All of the consequences for prosocial responding to refusals should be identified as things the student likes and all of the consequences for antisocial responding to refusals should be identified as things the student dislikes.

6. Beliefs

Beliefs Assessment: See pages 88–89 in Appendix A.

7. Perceives Solutions

Problem Solving: Using the target student's own experiences, make up at least two problem situations involving refusals (e.g., "You want to use the swings at recess but all of them are being used. You ask each person if you can have a turn and they all refuse you. You still want to use the swings but they won't give you a turn. Think of as many things as you can that you could do to solve this problem."). For a solution to be considered acceptable, it must meet the following criteria:

(a) It is effective (i.e., it would solve the target student's problem without creating more or different problems for him or her);

(b) it is feasible (i.e., it is something that the target student could actually do); and

(c) it is prosocial (i.e., behavior that would be considered acceptable by the school).

CAP: At least two acceptable solutions for each problem.

6. Verbally/Physically Intimidates Others to Meet Demands

EXTORT

Student _____ Evaluator _____ Date _____

MALADAPTIVE BEHAVIOR: Student makes requests of others in the form of a demand and threatens a negative consequence if compliance is refused or delayed.

Prerequisites	Status		
	Y	N	?
1. Understands that when he or she makes request of others, he or she *is expected* to do so in a prosocial way (i.e., ask, not demand, and repeat request or accept when refused).	☐	☐	☐
2. *Is aware* of when he or she is making request of others in a prosocial and an antisocial way.	☐	☐	☐
3. There are no factors (e.g., anger) currently *beyond the student's control* that would make it difficult for him or her to make requests in a prosocial way.	☐	☐	☐
4. *Has skills and knowledge* needed to make requests in a prosocial way.	☐	☐	☐
5. *Considers consequences* of making requests in a prosocial way more rewarding (or less aversive) than responding in an antisocial way.	☐	☐	☐
6. Does not hold any *beliefs incompatible* with making requests of others in a prosocial way.	☐	☐	☐

6. Verbally/Physically Intimidates Others to Meet Demands (*Continued*)

EXTORT

TARGET BEHAVIOR: Student makes requests of others in a prosocial way by asking, not demanding, and, if refused, repeating request or accepting refusal.

Assessment (use only if status is ?)	Results	Intervention (use only if status is N)
ask student (see p. 54, #1)	_____ _____	direct instruction (see pp. 75, 110)
simultaneous monitoring (see p. 54, #2)	_____ _____	self-monitoring (see pp. 76, 110–111)
peer comparison (see p. 54, #3)	_____ _____	stress inoculation for anger (see pp. 76, 112)
role play test (see p. 55, #4)	_____ _____	social skills training (see pp. 76, 111)
cue-sort exercise (see p. 55, #5)	_____ _____ _____	verbal mediation (see pp. 76, 112) behavior modification (see pp. 75, 109)
beliefs assessment (see p. 56, #6)	_____ _____	cognitive restructuring (see pp. 75, 109–110)

Assessments—EXTORT

1. Expectation

Ask Student: Read only boldface material to student. **"Tell me in your own words what you are supposed to do when you want someone to do something for you."** His or her answer should convey the idea that he or she is expected to ask (not demand) and not threaten a negative consequence if compliance is refused or delayed. Instead, he or she should repeat the request or accept the refusal. If the student has difficulty supplying a correct response, switch to a select-response format (see p. 12 of this manual).

CAP: Answers correctly with little or no prompting within 10 seconds of being asked.

2. Awareness

Simultaneous Monitoring: You and the student simultaneously (but separately) monitor the frequency of his or her prosocial and antisocial requests of others using the following procedure:

(a) Choose an interval of time when the target student is likely to make requests of others (e.g., free time or during a group activity) and it is relatively easy for you to monitor his or her behavior.

(b) Apply a strip of masking tape around your wrist and one around the student's wrist.

(c) Explain to the student what you want him or her to do. Say, **"For the next** (you decide how long) **minutes, I want you to keep track of how you make requests of others. If you ask (rather than demand) without threats, I want you to mark a + on your wrist tape.** (Model for student.) **If you demand (rather than ask) and threaten to hurt the person unless you get what you want from him or her, I want you to mark a 0 on your tape.** (Model for student.) **Now tell me what you are supposed to do."**

(d) Set a timer to signal the end of the monitoring trial and cue the student to begin monitoring.

(e) Position yourself in the room so that you can observe the student but he or she cannot observe you, and begin monitoring in the manner described above.

(f) If the student does not record his or her behavior on his or her tape when he or she should, you may *remind the student once*, but do not tell him or her what to record. He or she needs to decide that for him- or herself.

(g) Continue until the timer signals the end of the monitoring trial. Cue the student to stop monitoring and remove his or her wrist tape.

(h) Repeat steps (a) through (g) for two additional trials (may be same day or next).

(i) Calculate the percentage of agreement between your data and the target student's data by adding up the total number of 0's *on all three* of your tapes and the total number of 0's *on all three* of the student's tapes. Divide the larger total into the smaller total and multiply by 100.

CAP: At least 80% interobserver agreement between the teacher's data and the student's data.

3. Self-Control

Peer Comparison: Use Table 1.3 to help select a small ($N = 2$–3) sample of students, some with observable signs of anger and some without. Choose one or more of the anger signs listed in the table to monitor, and use the following procedure:

(a) Choose a time when the target student and the peer sample can be monitored at the same time, during an activity that typically elicits anger in the students, preferably when they are not moving around (e.g., class discussion or lesson).

(b) Use a monitoring form similar to the example in Figure 3.2.

(c) As unobtrusively as possible, both you *and a second observer* (teaching partner, assistant, psychologist) glance at each student *one at a time (in the same order)* for a 10-second interval (either count to yourself or set the timer on your watch). If the student you are watching engages in one or more of the anger signs you are monitoring *at any time* during that interval, record a mark (/) in a box next to the student's name. Then move on to the next student, observe and record for 10 seconds, move on to the next student, observe and record for 10 seconds, move on to the next student, and so on. Make sure that you and the second observer do not look at each other's monitoring forms. When you finish with the last student, start all over again.

(d) Continue to observe and record in this manner until you have at least 12 intervals completed for each student.

(e) Compute the percentage of interobserver agreement between your data and those of the second observer by finding the total number of anger signs (/) each of you recorded and dividing the larger total into the smaller total. Assuming there is at least 80% agreement between you and the second observer on the first monitoring trial, repeat steps (a) through (e) for two more trials, preferably over 2 different days. If there is less than 80% agreement, refer to page 15 of this manual before proceeding.

(f) Find the median for each student's three trial scores and compare the target student's median with the median scores for each of the students in the peer sample.

CAP: The target student's data (i.e., median score) more closely resemble the data (i.e., median scores) of nonangry peers than those of the angry peers. See page 107 of this manual for additional anger assessments.

4. Competence

Role Play Test: You may change any or all of the role play situations below if they are not age appropriate for your student(s), the vocabulary is too difficult, or the situations are unrealistic.

(a) Read only boldface material to the student. Say, **"I want you to role-play (act out) with me how you would request (ask for) something from another person in a prosocial (acceptable) way. Don't tell me what you would do; *show me*."** In each case, write down what the student says and/or does.

(b) **"I'm a student sitting next to you in class and you want to get a pencil from me. Show me how you would ask me for a pencil in an acceptable way."** (The target student should make a request first; then you refuse; the student should repeat the request at least two more times; you refuse each time; wait to see what the student does the last time you refuse him or her; if the student does nothing, prompt him or her [e.g., **"Come on. You want a pencil. I've refused you three times. Show me what you would do."**]).

(c) **"I'm a student on the playground playing with a basketball and you want a chance to use it. Show me how you would try to get the ball from me in an acceptable way."** (The target student should make a request first; then you refuse; continue as in [b] above).

(d) **"You want me to give you some money for lunch. Show me how you would try to get some money from me."** (The target student should make a request first; then you refuse; continue as in [b] above).

CAP: The student (in your judgment) is able to demonstrate (i.e., role-play) a prosocial request in the three situations without any prompting from you.

A "prosocial request" requires that the student does *all* of the following:

- The student poses his or her initial request as a question (e.g., "John, you got a pencil I can use?") in a neutral (nonthreatening) tone of voice, facial expression, and body posture.
- If the student's first request is granted, he or she expresses pleasure or appreciation (e.g., "Thanks.").
- If the student's first request is denied, he or she repeats the request at least two more times in a neutral (nonthreatening) way (as above).
- If the student's last request is denied, he or she accepts without incident.

5. Motivation

Cue Sort: You will need some blank 3 × 5 cards to write on. Read only boldface material to the student.

(a) To see if the student knows the consequences of making *prosocial* requests (i.e., asking and either repeating requests and/or accepting refusals), ask him or her, **"What happens to you when you ask someone to do something, they refuse to do it, and you accept his or her refusal?"** Write the student's responses on 3 × 5 cards, one response to a card.

(b) If the student has difficulty supplying a correct response, switch to a select-response format (see p. 12 of this manual). Write the student's responses on 3 × 5 cards, one response to a card. Indicate on the back of each card whether the student supplied the consequence or you supplied it.

(c) If the student continues to have difficulty, tell him or her what the consequences are and write them down on the cards.

(d) To see if the student knows the consequences of making *antisocial* requests (i.e., demanding and threatening negative consequences for refusal or delay), ask him or her: **"What happens to you when you demand something from someone and threaten to hurt that person if he or she refuses (or is slow) to do what you want?"** Write down these responses on 3 × 5 cards, one response to a card.

(e) Follow the same procedures as above if the student doesn't name all of the negative consequences.

(f) When all of the consequences have been written down, shuffle the cards.

(g) Give the cards to the student and ask him or her to sort them according to likes and dislikes. Say, **"Here are some things that happen to you in school when you respond to refusals in an acceptable way and in an unacceptable way. Sort them into two groups—things you like and things you dislike."** Help the student get started by modeling what you want him or her to do. Help the student read some or all of the cards if necessary. If he or she can't make up his or her mind about a consequence, put it in a third pile.

CAP: All of the consequences for making requests in a pro-social way should be identified as things the student likes and all of the consequences for making requests in an antisocial way should be identified as things the student dislikes.

6. Beliefs

Beliefs Assessment: See pages 90–91 in Appendix A.

7. Destroys Property of Others

DEST PROP

Student _____ Evaluator _____ Date _____

MALADAPTIVE BEHAVIOR: Student handles property of others in a destructive way (i.e., not as it was designed to be handled—intentionally trying to damage it).

Prerequisites	Status		
	Y	N	?
1. Understands that he or she *is expected* to handle the property of others in a nondestructive way.	☐	☐	☐
2. *Is aware* of when he or she is handling property of others in both destructive and nondestructive ways.	☐	☐	☐
3. There are no factors (e.g., anger, impulsivity) currently *beyond the student's control* that would make it difficult for him or her to handle the property of others in nondestructive way.	☐	☐	☐
4. *Has skills and knowledge* needed to handle property of others in nondestructive way.	☐	☐	☐
5. *Considers consequences* of handling others' property in nondestructive way more rewarding (or less aversive) than handling it in a destructive way.	☐	☐	☐
6. Does not hold any *beliefs incompatible* with handling property of others in nondestructive way.	☐	☐	☐

7. Destroys Property of Others (*Continued*)

TARGET BEHAVIOR: Student will handle property of others in a nondestructive way (i.e., as it was intended, without trying to harm it).

Assessment (use only if status is ?)	Results	Intervention (use only if status is N)
ask student (see p. 59, #1)	_____ _____	direct instruction (see pp. 75, 110)
simultaneous estimation (see p. 59, #2)	_____ _____	self-monitoring (see pp. 76, 110–111)
peer comparison (see p. 59, #3)	_____ _____ _____ _____	stress inoculation for anger (see pp. 76, 112) self-instructional training for impulsivity (see pp. 76, 110)
skills test (see pp. 59–60, #4)	_____ _____	direct instruction (see pp. 75, 110)
cue-sort exercise (see p. 60, #5)	_____ _____ _____ _____	verbal mediation (see pp. 76, 112) behavior modification (see pp. 75, 109)
beliefs assessment (see p. 60, #6)	_____ _____	cognitive restructuring (see pp. 75, 109–110)

Assessments—DEST PROP

1. Expectation

Ask Student: Read only boldface material to the student. **"Tell me in your own words how you are supposed to handle someone else's property."** The student's answer should convey the idea that he or she is expected to handle property of others the way it was intended to be handled and without trying to damage it. If the student has difficulty supplying a correct response, switch to a select-response format (see p. 12 of this manual).

CAP: Answering correctly with little or no prompting within 10 seconds of being asked.

2. Awareness

Simultaneous Estimation: Destructive behavior needs to be interrupted at its earliest appearance. Because any environmental cue draws the student's attention to the behavior he or she is engaging in, it is difficult to reliably assess the student's awareness of it on his or her own. Whenever a prerequisite cannot be reliably assessed, you should assume that the student lacks that prerequisite or use the following procedure:

(a) Monitor the frequency of destructive behaviors in the target student over a predetermined interval of time.

(b) At the end of this interval, ask the student how many times he or she thinks he or she engaged in destructive behavior.

(c) Compute the percentage of agreement by using your data and the student's data and dividing the larger amount into the smaller and multiplying that number by 100. Repeat this procedure for two more intervals.

CAP: At least 80% interobserver agreement between your data and the student's data on at least two of the three intervals.

3. Self-Control

Peer Comparison: Use Table 1.3 to help select a small (N = 2–3) sample of students, some with observable signs of anger and some without. Choose one or more of the anger signs listed in the table to monitor, and use the following procedure:

(a) Choose a time for monitoring when the target student and the peer sample can be monitored at the

same time, during an activity that typically elicits anger in the students, preferably when they are not moving around (e.g., class discussion or lesson).

(b) Use a monitoring form similar to the example in Figure 3.2.

(c) As unobtrusively as possible, both you *and a second observer* (teaching partner, assistant, psychologist) glance at each student *one at a time (in the same order)* for a 10-second interval (either count to yourself or set the timer on your watch). If the student you are watching engages in one or more of the anger signs you are monitoring *at any time during that interval*, record a mark (/) in a box next to the student's name. Then move on to the next student, observe and record for 10 seconds, and so on. Make sure that you and the second observer do not look at each other's monitoring forms. When you finish with the last student, start all over again.

(d) Continue to observe and record in this manner until you have at least 12 intervals completed for each student.

(e) Compute the percentage of interobserver agreement between your data and the data of the second observer by finding the total number of anger signs (/) each of you recorded and dividing the larger total into the smaller total. Assuming there is at least 80% agreement between you and the second observer on the first monitoring trial, repeat steps (a) through (e) for two more trials, preferably over 2 different days. If the percentage of agreement is less than 80%, refer to page 15 of this manual before proceeding.

(f) Find the median for each student's three trial scores and compare the target student's median with the median scores for each of the students in the peer sample.

CAP: The target student's data (i.e., median score) more closely resemble the data (i.e., median scores) of nonangry peers than the data of the angry peers. See page 107 of this manual for additional anger assessments.

Use the same procedure and the same type of monitoring form to monitor the frequency of impulsivity in the target student and a small sample of peers, some with impulse control and some without. Use Table 1.3 to help you select the peer sample and the observable signs of impulsivity to monitor.

CAP: The target student's data (i.e., median score) more closely resemble data (i.e., median scores) of the nonimpulsive peers than the data of the impulsive peers. See page 108 of this manual for additional impulsivity assessments.

4. Competence

Skills Test: You want to assess the target student's skills at handling other people's property in the manner for which it was intended.

(a) Supply the student with materials such as books, crayons, pencils, and so on, belonging to the school and/or his or her peers, and ask the student to use these objects for a period of time.

(b) Say, **"I would like you to use (handle) this** (name of object or material) **for the next** (amount of time)**. Show me how you can use (handle) it without damaging it."**

CAP: Uses the material as it was intended to be used and handles it without damaging it (i.e., it is returned to the owner in same or similar condition as it was received).

5. Motivation

Cue Sort: You will need some blank 3 × 5 cards to write on. Read only boldface material to the student.

(a) To see if the student knows the consequences of socially appropriate responding to refusals, ask him or her, **"What happens to you when you handle other people's property in a way that does not harm it?"** Write the student's responses on 3 × 5 cards, one response to a card.

(b) If the student has difficulty supplying a correct response, switch to a select-response format (see p. 12 of this manual). Write the student's responses on 3 × 5 cards, one response to a card. Indicate on the back of each card whether the student supplied the consequence or you supplied it.

(c) If the student continues to have difficulty, tell him or her what the consequences are and write them down on the cards.

(d) To see if the student knows the consequences of handling other people's property in a destructive way, ask him or her, **"What happens to you when you handle other people's property in a way that harms it?"** Write the student's responses on 3 × 5 cards, one response to a card.

(e) Follow the same procedures as in (c) if the student doesn't name all of the negative consequences.

(f) When all of the consequences have been written down, shuffle the cards.

(g) Give the cards to the student and ask him or her to sort them according to likes and dislikes. Say, **"Here are some things that happen to you in school. Sort them into two groups—things you like and things you dislike."** Help the student read the cards if necessary.

CAP: All of the consequences for handling other people's property in a nondestructive way should be identified as things the student likes and all of the consequences for handling it in a destructive way should be identified as things the student dislikes.

6. Beliefs

Beliefs Assessment: See pages 92–93 in Appendix A.

8. Responds Aggressively to Peer Provocation

AGG/PROV

Student _____   Evaluator _____   Date _____

MALADAPTIVE BEHAVIOR: Student responds to peer provocation (i.e., teasing, threats, swearing, insults, disapproval) with aggression (i.e., verbally and/or physically attacking peers).

Prerequisites	Status Y	N	?
1. Understands that when provoked by peers, he or she *is expected* to respond without any verbal or physical aggression.	☐	☐	☐
2. *Is aware* of when he or she is responding to peer provocation assertively and when he or she is responding aggressively.	☐	☐	☐
3. There are no factors (e.g., anger and/or impulsivity) currently *beyond the student's control* that would make it difficult for him or her to respond assertively, without any aggression, to peer provocation.	☐	☐	☐
4. *Has skills and knowledge* needed to respond to peer provocation assertively without aggression.	☐	☐	☐
5. *Considers consequences* of responding to peer provocation assertively and without aggression more rewarding (or less aversive) than responding with aggression.	☐	☐	☐
6. Does not hold any *beliefs incompatible* with responding to peer provocation assertively without aggression.	☐	☐	☐
7. *Perceives* assertive responding as a possible solution to the problem of peer provocation.	☐	☐	☐

8. Responds Aggressively to Peer Provocation (*Continued*)

TARGET BEHAVIOR: When provoked by peers (i.e., teasing, threats, insulting, swearing, disapproval), the student responds assertively (i.e., tells peers to stop and what he or she feels about their behavior), without being aggressive.

Assessment (use only if status is ?)	Results	Intervention (use only if status is N)
ask student (see p. 63, #1)	_____ _____	direct instruction (see pp. 75, 110)
simultaneous estimation (see p. 63, #2)	_____ _____	self-monitoring (see pp. 76, 110–111)
peer comparison (see p. 63, #3)	_____ _____ _____	stress inoculation for anger (see pp. 76, 112) self-instructional training for impulsivity (see pp. 76, 110)
role play test (see p. 64, #4)	_____ _____	social skills training (see pp. 76, 111)
cue-sort exercise (see p. 64, #5)	_____ _____ _____	verbal mediation (see pp. 76, 112) behavior modification (see pp. 75, 109)
beliefs assessment (see p. 64, #6)	_____ _____	cognitive restructuring (see pp. 75, 109–110)
generates solutions (see p. 65, #7)	_____ _____	problem solving (see pp. 76, 110)

Assessments—AGG/PROV

1. Expectation

Ask Student: Read only boldface material to the student. **"Tell me in your own words what you are supposed to do when someone teases you (threatens you, calls you a name, makes fun of you, puts you down) at school."** The student's answer should convey the idea that he or she knows that he or she is expected to be assertive (i.e., tell them to stop and what he or she feels) without any aggressive behavior. If the student has difficulty supplying a correct response, switch to a select-response format (see p. 12 of this manual).

CAP: Answering correctly with little or no prompting within 10 seconds of being asked.

2. Awareness

Simultaneous Estimation: Aggressive behavior (like destructive behavior) needs to be interrupted at its earliest appearance. Because any environmental intervention draws the student's attention to the behavior he or she is engaging in, it is difficult to reliably assess his or her awareness of it on his or her own. Whenever a prerequisite cannot be reliably assessed, you should assume that the student lacks that prerequisite or use the following procedure:

(a) Draw a number of boxes on a piece of masking tape and apply the tape to your wrist.

(b) Each time the student is provoked, record his or her response in one of the boxes. If he or she responds aggressively (i.e., verbally or physically attacks peers), record a 0 and intervene if necessary. If he or she responds assertively (i.e., tells them to stop and what he or she feels), record a + and ignore or verbally praise.

(c) When all of the boxes on your wrist tape are filled, tell the student how many times he or she was teased and ask him or her how many times he or she thinks he or she responded assertively and aggressively (use vocabulary appropriate for student).

(d) Repeat steps (a) through (c) for two additional trials over the course of 2 or more days.

(e) Using *your* data, compute the percentages of assertive responding for each of the three monitoring trials by dividing the total number of +'s and 0's per trial into the total number of +'s per trial and

multiply this number by 100. Help the student compute his or her percentage of assertive responding using his or her estimated data.

(f) Compare your percentage of assertive responding to the student's percentage.

CAP: Not less than 10% difference between your data and the student's data on at least two of the three intervals.

3. Self-Control

Peer Comparison: Use Table 1.3 to help select a small ($N = 2$–3) sample of students, some with observable signs of anger and some without. Choose one or more of the anger signs listed in the table to monitor, and use the following procedure:

(a) Choose a time for monitoring when the target student and the peer sample can be monitored at the same time, during an activity that typically elicits anger in the students, preferably when they are not moving around (e.g., class discussion or lesson).

(b) Use a monitoring form similar to the example in Figure 3.2.

(c) As unobtrusively as possible, both you *and a second observer* (teaching partner, assistant, psychologist) glance at each student *one at a time (in the same order)* for a 10-second interval (either count to yourself or set the timer on your watch). If the student you are watching engages in one or more of the anger signs you are monitoring *at any time during that interval*, record a mark (/) in a box next to the student's name. Then move on to the next student, and so on. Make sure that you and the second observer do not look at each other's monitoring forms. When you finish with the last student, start all over again.

(d) Continue to observe and record in this manner until you have at least 12 intervals completed for each student.

(e) Compute the percentage of interobserver agreement between your data and those of the second observer by finding the total number of anger signs (/) each of you recorded and dividing the larger total into the smaller total. Assuming there is at least 80% agreement between you and the second observer on the first monitoring trial, repeat steps (a) through (d) for two more trials, preferably over 2 different days. If the percentage of agreement is less than 80%, refer to page 15 of this manual before proceeding.

(f) Find the median for each student's three trial scores and compare the target student's median with the median scores for each of the students in the peer sample.

CAP: *The target student's data (i.e., median score) more closely resemble the data (i.e., median scores) of the nonangry peers than those of the angry peers.*

Use the same procedure and the same type of monitoring form to monitor the frequency of impulsivity in the target student and a small sample of peers, some with impulse control and some without. Use Table 1.3 to help you select the peer sample and the observable signs of impulsivity to monitor.

CAP: *The target student's data (i.e., median score) more closely resemble data (i.e., median scores) of the nonimpulsive peers than the data of the impulsive peers.* See page 108 of this manual for additional impulsivity assessments.

4. Competence

Role Play Test: You may change any or all of the role play situations below if they are not age appropriate for your student(s), the vocabulary is too difficult, or the situations are unrealistic.

(a) Read only boldface material to student. Say, **"I want you to role-play (act out) with me how you would be assertive in each of the following situations. Don't tell me what you would do; *show me*."** In each case, write down what the student says and/or does.

(b) **"You are on the playground and I come up to you and call you a name. Show me how you would act assertively."** (Try to act as if you and the target student are actually on a playground; call him or her a name you know he or she won't like; wait for a response.)

(c) **"You and I are walking in the hall and I make fun of the way you walk. Show me how you would act assertively."** (Try to act as if you and the target student are actually walking down the hall; make fun of his or her walking; wait for a response.)

(d) **"You ask the teacher a question in class and I say something negative (bad) about it for everybody to hear. Show me how you would act assertively."** (The target student asks a question; you say, **"What a dumb question!"** Wait for his or her response.)

CAP: *The student (in your judgment) is able to demonstrate (i.e., role-play) an assertive response in at least two of the three*

situations without any prompting from you. An "assertive response" requires that the student remain composed (no visible signs of anger or anxiety), make direct eye contact, keep hands at sides, and say, "Don't say (or do) that. I don't like it"—using a firm but conversational tone of voice without any aggressive behavior (e.g., body posturing, cursing, threatening, or making physical contact).

5. Motivation

Cue Sort: You will need some blank 3 × 5 cards to write on. Read only boldface material to the student.

(a) To see if the student knows the consequences of assertive responding to peer provocation, ask him or her, **"What happens to you when you act assertively (tell others to stop and tell what you feel) when they pick on (tease, bother) you?"** Write the student's responses on 3 × 5 cards, one response to a card.

(b) If the student has difficulty supplying a correct response, switch to a select-response format (see p. 12 of this manual). Write the student's responses on 3 × 5 cards, one response to a card. Indicate on the back of each card whether the student supplied the consequence or you supplied it.

(c) If the student continues to have difficulty, tell him or her what the consequences are and write them on the cards.

(d) To see if the student knows the consequences of aggressive responding to peer provocation, ask him or her, **"What happens to you when you yell and curse at others and threaten or try to hurt them when they pick on (tease, bother) you?"** Write the student's responses on 3 × 5 cards, one response to a card.

(e) Follow the same procedures as in (c) if the student doesn't name all of the negative consequences.

(f) When all of the consequences have been written down, shuffle the cards.

(g) Give the cards to the student and ask him or her to sort them according to likes and dislikes. Say, **"These are some things that happen to you in school. Sort them into two groups—things you like and things you dislike."** Help the student get started by modeling what you want him or her to do. Help the student read the cards if necessary. If he or she can't make up his or her mind about a consequence, put it in a third pile.

CAP: All of the consequences for assertive responding should be identified as things the student likes and all of the consequences for aggressive responding should be identified as things the student dislikes.

6. Beliefs

Beliefs Assessment: See pages 94–95 in Appendix A.

7. Perceives Solutions

Problem Solving: Using the target student's own experiences, make up at least two problem situations involving peer provocation (e.g., "Some of your classmates laugh at you whenever you try to answer a question in class. You want them to stop. Think of as many things as you can that you could do to solve this problem."). To be acceptable, a solution must satisfy the following conditions:

- It is effective (i.e., it would solve the target student's problem without creating more or different problems).

- It is feasible (i.e., it is something that the target student could actually do).

- It is prosocial (i.e., a behavior that would be considered acceptable by the school).

CAP: The student generates at least two acceptable solutions for each problem.

9. Verbally Aggressive Without Provocation

VERB AGG/NO PROV

Student _____ Evaluator _____ Date _____

MALADAPTIVE BEHAVIOR: When interacting with peers, student is verbally aggressive (e.g., teasing, threatening, cursing, insulting, disapproving) without provocation.

Prerequisites	Status		
	Y	N	?
1. Understands that he or she *is expected* to interact with peers in a prosocial way, without any verbally aggressive behavior.	☐	☐	☐
2. *Is aware* of when he or she is interacting with peers in a prosocial and in a verbally aggressive way.	☐	☐	☐
3. There are no factors (e.g., anger or impulsivity) currently *beyond the student's control* that would make it difficult for him or her to interact with peers in a prosocial way without any verbally aggressive behavior.	☐	☐	☐
4. *Has skills and knowledge* needed to interact with peers in a prosocial way without any verbally aggressive behavior.	☐	☐	☐
5. *Considers consequences* of interacting with peers in a prosocial way, without verbal aggression, more rewarding (or less aversive) than being verbally aggressive.	☐	☐	☐
6. Does not hold any *beliefs incompatible* with interacting with peers in a prosocial way without any verbally aggressive behavior.	☐	☐	☐

9. Verbally Aggressive Without Provocation (*Continued*)

TARGET BEHAVIOR: Student interacts with peers in a prosocial manner (e.g., making positive or neutral comments without swearing, insulting, disapproving, threatening, or teasing).

Assessment (use only if status is ?)	Results	Intervention (use only if status is N)
ask student (see p. 68, #1)	_____ _____	direct instruction (see pp. 75, 110)
simultaneous estimation (see p. 68, #2)	_____ _____	self-monitoring (see pp. 76, 110–111)
peer comparison (see p. 68, #3)	_____ _____	stress inoculation for anger (see pp. 76, 112) self-instructional training for impulsivity (see pp. 76, 110)
social skills assessment (see p. 69, #4)	_____ _____	social skills training (see pp. 76, 111)
cue-sort exercise (see p. 69, #5)	_____ _____	verbal mediation (see pp. 76, 112) behavior modification (see pp. 75, 109)
beliefs assessment (see p. 69, #6)	_____ _____	cognitive restructuring (see pp. 75, 109–110)

Assessments—VERB AGG/NO PROV

1. Expectation

Ask Student: Read only boldface material to the student. **"Tell me in your own words how you are supposed to interact with (talk to) your classmates here at school."** The student's answer should convey the idea that he or she knows that he or she is expected to interact in a prosocial way (i.e., make positive or neutral comments to peers without any teasing, threatening, insulting, swearing, or disapproving). If student has difficulty supplying a correct response, switch to a select-response format (see p. 12 of this manual).

CAP: Answering correctly with little or no prompting within 10 seconds of being asked.

2. Awareness

Simultaneous Estimation: Aggressive behavior (like destructive behavior) needs to be interrupted at its earliest appearance. Because any environmental intervention draws the student's attention to the behavior he or she is engaging in, it is difficult to reliably assess the student's awareness of it on his or her own. Whenever a prerequisite cannot be reliably assessed, you should assume that the student lacks that prerequisite or use the following procedure:

(a) Monitor the frequency of verbally aggressive behaviors (i.e., teasing, threatening, insulting, disapproving, or swearing) in the target student over a predetermined interval of time by making a mark (/) on a piece of masking tape applied to your wrist.

(b) Continue to monitor the behavior in this fashion until it is time to stop.

(c) Ask the student to estimate how many times he or she thinks he or she engaged in the verbally aggressive behavior (use specific behaviors, e.g., teasing).

(d) Compute the percentage of agreement between your data and the student's estimated data by dividing the larger amount into the smaller amount and multiplying this by 100. Repeat this procedure for two more intervals.

CAP: At least 80% agreement between your data and the student's data on at least two of the three intervals.

3. Self-Control

Peer Comparison: Use Table 1.3 to help select a small (N = 2–3) sample of students, some with observable signs of anger and some without. Choose one or more of the anger signs listed in the table to monitor, and use the following procedure:

(a) Choose a time for monitoring when the target student and the peer sample can be monitored at the same time, during an activity that typically elicits anger in the students, preferably when they are not moving around (e.g., class discussion or lesson).

(b) Use a monitoring form similar to the example shown in Figure 3.2.

(c) As unobtrusively as possible, both you *and a second observer* (teaching partner, assistant, psychologist) glance at each student *one at a time (in the same order)* for a 10-second interval (either count to yourself or set the timer on your watch). If the student you are watching engages in one or more of the anger signs you are monitoring at any time during that interval, record a mark (/) in a box next to the student's name. Then move on to the next student, observe and record for 10 seconds, move on to the next student, observe and record for 10 seconds, and so on. Make sure that you and the second observer do not look at each other's monitoring forms. When you finish with the last student, start all over again.

(d) Continue to observe and record in this manner until you have at least 12 intervals completed for each student.

(e) Compute the percentage of interobserver agreement between your data and those of the second observer by finding the total number of anger signs (/) each of you recorded and dividing the larger total into the smaller total. Assuming there is at least 80% agreement between you and the second observer on the first monitoring trial, repeat steps (a) through (d) for two more trials, preferably over 2 different days. If the percentage of agreement is less than 80%, refer to page 15 of this manual before proceeding.

(f) Find the median for each student's three trial scores and compare the target student's median with the median scores for each of the students in the peer sample.

CAP: The target student's data (i.e., median score) more closely resemble the data (i.e., median scores) of nonangry peers than the data of the angry peers. See page 107 of this manual for additional anger assessments.

Use the procedure above to monitor the frequency of impulsivity in the target student and in a small sample of peers, some with signs of impulsivity and some without.

CAP: The target student's data (i.e., median scores) more closely resemble the data (median scores) of the nonimpulsive peers than the data of the impulsive peers. See page 108 of this manual for additional impulsivity assessments.

4. Competence

Social Skills Assessment: Complete a social skills assessment (see Appendix C, p. 109). Examine especially those skills needed for prosocial interaction with peers (e.g., giving and receiving compliments).

CAP: Passes assessment.

5. Motivation

Cue Sort: You will need some blank 3 × 5 cards to write on. Read only boldface material to the student.

(a) To see if the student knows the consequences of interacting with peers in a prosocial way, ask him or her, **"What happens to you when you talk to peers in a friendly, approving way without threatening, insulting, cursing, or disapproving of them?"** Write the student's responses on 3 × 5 cards, one response to a card.

(b) If the student has difficulty supplying the consequences of prosocial interaction, switch to a select-response format (see p. 12 of this manual). If the student continues to have difficulty, tell him or her the consequences and write them down on the cards. Indicate on the back of each card whether the student named the consequences or you did.

(c) To see if the student knows the consequences of interacting with peers in an antisocial way, ask him or her, **"What happens to you when you threaten, shame, curse, or disapprove of your peers?"** Write the student's responses on 3 × 5 cards, one response to a card. Follow the same procedure as in (b) if the student doesn't name all of the consequences of antisocial interactions.

(d) When all of the consequences have been written down, shuffle the cards.

(e) Give the cards to the student and ask him or her to sort them according to likes and dislikes. Say, **"Here are some things that happen to you in school. Sort them into two groups—things you like and things you dislike."** Help the student get started by modeling what you want him or her to do. Help the student read the cards if necessary. If he or she can't make up his or her mind about a consequence, have him or her put the card in a third pile.

CAP: All of the consequences for talking to peers in a prosocial way should be identified as things the student likes and all the consequences for talking to peers in an antisocial way should be identified as things the student dislikes.

6. Beliefs

Beliefs Assessment: See pages 96–97 in Appendix A.

10. Physically Aggressive Without Provocation

PHYS AGG/NO PROV

Student _____ Evaluator _____ Date _____

MALADAPTIVE BEHAVIOR: When interacting with peers, student engages in physically aggressive behavior (hitting, slapping, kicking, biting, pushing, grabbing) without provocation.

Prerequisites	Status		
	Y	N	?
1. Understands that he or she *is expected* to interact with peer group in a prosocial way, without any physically aggressive behavior.	☐	☐	☐
2. *Is aware* of when he or she is interacting with peers in a prosocial way and in an antisocial way.	☐	☐	☐
3. There are no factors (e.g., anger or impulsivity) currently *beyond the student's control* that might make it difficult for him or her to interact with peers in a prosocial way without any physically aggressive behavior.	☐	☐	☐
4. *Has skills and knowledge* needed to interact with peers in a prosocial way without any physically aggressive behavior.	☐	☐	☐
5. *Considers consequences* of interacting with peers in a prosocial way, without physical aggression, more rewarding (or less aversive) than being physically aggressive.	☐	☐	☐
6. Does not hold any *beliefs incompatible* with interacting with peers in a prosocial way without any physically aggressive behavior.	☐	☐	☐

10. Physically Aggressive Without Provocation (*Continued*)

TARGET BEHAVIOR: Student will interact with peers in a prosocial manner without any physical aggression (e.g., hitting, slapping, kicking).

Assessment (use only if status is ?)	Results	Intervention (use only if status is N)
ask student (see p. 72, #1)	_____ _____	direct instruction (see pp. 75, 110)
simultaneous estimation (see p. 72, #2)	_____ _____	self-monitoring (see pp. 76, 110–111)
peer comparison (see p. 72, #3)	_____ _____ _____ _____	stress inoculation for anger (see pp. 76, 112) self-instructional training for impulsivity (see pp. 76, 110)
social skills test (see p. 73, #4)	_____ _____	social skills training (see pp. 76, 111)
cue-sort exercise (see p. 73, #5)	_____ _____ _____	verbal mediation (see pp. 76, 112) behavior modification (see pp. 75, 109)
beliefs assessment (see p. 73, #6)	_____ _____	cognitive restructuring (see pp. 75, 109–110)

Assessments—PHYS AGG/NO PROV

1. Expectation

Ask Student: Read only boldface material to the student. **"Tell me in your own words how you are supposed to interact (behave) with your classmates here at school."** The student's answer should convey the idea that he or she knows that he or she is expected to interact in a prosocial way (i.e., without any physical aggression). If the student has difficulty supplying a correct response, switch to a select-response format (see p. 12 of this manual).

CAP: Answers correctly with little or no prompting within 10 seconds of being cued.

2. Awareness

Simultaneous Estimation: Aggressive behavior needs to be interrupted at its earliest appearance. Because any environmental cue draws the student's attention to the behavior he or she is engaging in, it is difficult to reliably assess the student's awareness of it on his or her own. Whenever a prerequisite cannot be reliably assessed, you should assume that the student lacks that prerequisite, or use the following procedure:

(a) Monitor the frequency of physically aggressive behaviors (e.g., hits, kicks, pushes) in the target student over a predetermined interval of time by making a mark (/) on a piece of masking tape applied to your wrist.

(b) Continue to monitor the behavior in this fashion until it is time to stop.

(c) Ask the student to estimate how many times he or she thinks he or she engaged in the physically aggressive behavior (use specific behaviors, e.g., punching, shoving).

(d) Compute the percentage of agreement between your data and the student's estimated data by dividing the larger amount into the smaller amount and multiplying this by 100. Repeat this procedure for two more intervals.

CAP: At least 80% agreement between your data and the student's data on at least two of the three intervals.

3. Self-Control

Peer Comparison: Use Table 1.3 to help select a small (N = 2–3) sample of students, some with observable signs of anger and some without. Choose one or more of the anger signs listed in the table to monitor, and use the following procedure:

(a) Choose a time for monitoring when the target student and the peer sample can be monitored at the same time, during an activity that typically elicits anger in the students, preferably when they are not moving around (e.g., class discussion or lesson).

(b) Use a monitoring form similar to the example shown in Figure 3.2.

(c) As unobtrusively as possible, both you *and a second observer* (teaching partner, assistant, psychologist) observe each student *one at a time (in the same order)* for a 10-second interval (either count to yourself or set the timer on your watch). If the student you are watching engages in one or more of the anger signs you are monitoring at any time during that interval, record a mark (/) in a box next to the student's name. Then move on to the next student, observe and record for 10 seconds, move on to the next student, observe and record for 10 seconds, and so on. Make sure that you and the second observer do not look at each other's monitoring forms. When you finish with the last student, start all over again.

(d) Continue to observe and record in this manner until you have at least 12 intervals completed for each student.

(e) Compute the percentage of interobserver agreement between your data and those of the second observer by finding the total number of anger signs (/) each of you recorded and dividing the larger total into the smaller total and multiplying by 100.

(f) Assuming there is at least 80% agreement between you and the second observer, repeat steps (a) through (e) for two more monitoring trials, preferably over 2 or more days.

(g) Find the median for each student's three trial scores and compare the target student's median with the median scores for each of the students in the peer sample.

CAP: The target student's data (i.e., median score) more closely resemble the data (i.e., median scores) of nonangry peers than the data of angry peers. See page 107 of this manual for additional anger assessments.

Use the same procedure and the same type of monitoring form to monitor the frequency of impulsivity in the target student and a small sample of peers, some with impulse control and some without. Use Table 1.3 to help you select the peer sample and the observable signs of impulsivity to monitor.

CAP: The target student's data (i.e., median score) more closely resemble data (i.e., median scores) of the nonimpulsive peers than the data of the impulsive peers. See page 108 of this manual for additional impulsivity assessments.

4. Competence

Social Skills Test: Complete a social skills assessment (see Appendix C, p. 109). Examine especially those skills needed for prosocial interaction with peers (e.g., being assertive, giving and receiving compliments).

CAP: Passes assessment.

5. Motivation

Cue Sort: You will need some blank 3 × 5 cards to write on. Read only boldface material to the student.

(a) To see if the student knows the consequences of interacting with peers in a prosocial way, ask him or her, **"What happens to you when you try to get along with your peers without fighting?"** Write the student's responses on 3 × 5 cards, one response to a card.

(b) If the student has difficulty supplying a correct response, switch to a select-response format (see

p. 12 of this manual). Write the student's responses on 3 × 5 cards, one response to a card. Indicate on the back of each card whether the student named the consequences or you did.

(c) If the student continues to have difficulty, tell him or her what the consequences are and write them down on the cards.

(d) To see if the student knows the consequences of interacting with peers in an antisocial way, ask him or her, **"What happens to you when you fight here at school?"** Write the student's responses on 3 × 5 cards, one response to a card.

(e) Follow the same procedure as in (c) if the student doesn't name all of the negative consequences.

(f) When all of the consequences have been written down, shuffle the cards.

(g) Give the cards to the student and ask him or her to sort them according to likes and dislikes. Say, **"Here are some things that happen to you in school. Sort them into two groups—things you like and things you dislike."** Help the student get started by modeling what you want him or her to do. Help the student read the cards if necessary. If he or she can't make up his or her mind about a consequence, put it in a third pile.

CAP: All of the consequences for interacting with peers in a prosocial manner should be identified as things the student likes and all the consequences for interacting with peers in an antisocial way should be identified as things the student dislikes.

6. Beliefs

Beliefs Assessment: See pages 98–99 in Appendix A.

Interventions

The best assessment tools not only tell you what's wrong, they also provide information about how to fix the problem. The column under the heading "Intervention" on the Beyond FA worksheets lists the type of intervention recommended for the remediation of the missing prerequisite(s) and where in the manual you can find information and resources regarding the intervention. The following interventions are presented in alphabetical order.

Behavior Modification: If the student is lacking the *motivation* prerequisite, you need to identify more powerful incentives so that he or she considers the consequences of engaging in the target behavior more rewarding than those of the maladaptive behavior. Try using an interest inventory (see Kaplan, 1995, *Beyond Behavior Modification;* and Appendix A) to identify these incentives. On the other hand, you might be using the right incentives but the wrong schedule of reinforcement. For example, using a continuous schedule of reinforcement (1:1) for too long can result in satiation in the student and a weakening of the target behavior, whereas not using it long enough can lead to a weakening of the target behavior through extinction. Another thing you might consider is latency, the time that elapses between the student's behavior and the presentation of the consequence. You may be taking too long to present the reward and the student is not able to make the connection between his or her behavior and its consequences. For more information on behavior modification as an intervention for strengthening behavior, see Chapter 5 in *Beyond Behavior Modification* (Kaplan, 1995).

Cognitive Restructuring: This intervention can be used if the student is lacking the *beliefs* prerequisite; it takes much longer than the other interventions because you are not simply trying to change the student's behavior, you are trying to change his or her belief system, something that has probably been with the student for many years. As noted earlier, it is essential to change the student's beliefs if you want him or her to internalize the target behavior, but such change is not essential for extrinsic (environmental) motivation. For information on imple-

menting cognitive restructuring, see Chapter 11 in *Beyond Behavior Modification* (Kaplan, 1995). Other valuable resources on cognitive restructuring may be found in Appendix C of this manual.

Direct Instruction: If the student is lacking the *expectation* prerequisite—the student does not understand what behavior is expected of him or her—you will need to teach the student the rules just like you might teach him or her spelling or phonics rules. According to the research on effective instruction, the best method of teaching most curriculum content to most students is direct instruction (Becker & Engelmann, 1973). For a simple explanation of direct instruction, refer to Price and Nelson (1999).

Environmental: This type of intervention should be used if the student is lacking the *self-control* prerequisite. Sometimes referred to as "environmental engineering," this type of intervention is typically the easiest and one of the most commonly used in schools. If the target student has difficulty controlling his or her *distractibility,* you might provide him or her with a study carrel and an audiotape and headset to listen to some quiet music. You can also purchase an inexpensive white noise machine to mask distracting class noise. Sometimes students with distractibility problems are understimulated rather than overstimulated. You might want to try keeping the student busy with work that provides enough stimulation that he or she doesn't feel compelled to create his or her own stimulation. If the student has difficulty controlling his or her *hyperactivity,* you can use environmental engineering to provide the space he or she needs to be hyperactive without disrupting the classroom. Provide the student with a safety "lane" around his or her desk where he or she can feel free to move about without creating a problem for you or the rest of the class. Do not attempt to restrict his or her movement, especially during learning activities. Have the student do his or her written work on an easel or on the blackboard, again in a noncongested area of the classroom. Try a buddy system or peer tutoring for the student who has trouble staying on task without supervision.

Direct involvement with peers can also benefit the student if he or she is depressed. There are any number of environmental modifications you can make to help students with self-control problems. You just need to exercise a little creativity and forethought.

Medical: Medical intervention is an option if the student is lacking the *self-control* prerequisite. If it appears that the student has a sensory impairment (e.g., vision or hearing loss), you need to bring this to the attention of his or her parents. Probably the most widely used medical intervention is the use of psychopharmacological drugs. Although there is some evidence that these drugs can provide relief in a wide range of disorders that inhibit self-control in children and youth, many professionals suggest trying behavioral and/or environmental interventions first. It goes without saying that failing such interventions, you should consider the use of safe and effective medication when appropriate.

Problem Solving: This intervention is to be used if a student is lacking the *perceiving solutions* prerequisite. Like cognitive restructuring, this prerequisite is not necessarily essential unless you want the student to internalize the target behavior. When you think he or she is ready for this intervention, see *Beyond Behavior Modification* (Kaplan, 1995, pp. 431–436). Other valuable resources on problem solving may be found in Appendix C.

Remedial: This intervention is to be used if the student is lacking the *competency* prerequisite. This type of intervention might focus on the mastery of academic skills or social skills (see social skills training on this page).

Self-Monitoring: Self-monitoring is to be used if a student is lacking the *awareness* prerequisite. One of the components of self-management, self-monitoring requires the student to keep a written record of his or her behavior, both maladaptive and target. Collecting data on one's own behavior increases one's awareness of it (see Kaplan, 1995, Chap. 9; and Workman & Katz, 1995).

Self-Instructional Training (SIT): This intervention is to be used if the student is lacking the *self-control* prerequisite. Not to be confused with self-monitoring, SIT is a structured form of self-talk that appears to be effective in the reduction of impulsivity (Meichenbaum, 1971, 1977; see also Kaplan, 1995, pp. 425–426).

Social Skills Training: To be used if a student is lacking the *competency* prerequisite. There are many fine commercially available social skills programs on the market. Many of these may be found in Appendix C. See also Chapter 10 in Kaplan (1995).

Stress Inoculation Training: This intervention may be effective if the student is lacking the *self-control* prerequisite. Stress inoculation training has been found to effectively relieve problems associated with depression, anxiety, and anger (Maag, 1988; Meichenbaum, 1985). It requires a lot of work on both your part and the student's, but it is well worth the effort (see Kaplan, 1995, pp. 459–465).

Verbal Mediation: This intervention should be used if the student is lacking the *motivation* prerequisite, especially if he or she has difficulty naming all of the consequences of the maladaptive and target behaviors (see Kaplan, 1995, pp. 428–429; and Workman & Katz, 1995, pp. 85–87).

Beliefs Assessments

Directions

Administering an Assessment

Before giving an assessment, read the directions as well as all of the items on the assessment you plan to use. Check the vocabulary to make sure it is appropriate for your student. Also make sure that the beliefs are expressed in a manner that is age appropriate for your student. Make any changes in vocabulary or content you deem necessary, *but be careful* not to change the idea conveyed in each item.

Determine the appropriate stimulus–response mode (e.g., student reads items and writes answers, student listens to items and writes answers, student listens to items and says answers).

Determine the appropriate time limit based on the stimulus–response mode and the student's abilities in receptive/expressive language. Do not give him or her so much time that he or she sits and vacillates back and forth between responses; nor should you give the student so little time that he or she feels rushed and marks any response without reflection.

Make sure the student understands the directions. He or she is supposed to answer "true" or "false" to each statement he or she reads (or is read to him or her). The student is not to leave any statements unanswered. If the student is undecided about a statement, encourage him or her to answer it one way or the other.

Scoring an Assessment

The purpose of the beliefs assessment is to determine whether or not a student endorses or holds a belief that is incompatible with engaging in the target behavior. There is no pass or fail on the beliefs assessments, and the student does not receive a quantitative (i.e., number) score of any kind.

Use the scoring key provided after each assessment to score the assessment. Statements suggestive of a belief that might be incompatible with the target behavior and/or supportive of the maladaptive behavior are *negative beliefs* and should be answered "false." Each negative belief has a corresponding (fair-pair) positive belief that might be incompatible with the maladaptive behavior, while supportive of the target behavior. All *positive beliefs* should be answered "true."

When the student gives the same answer (either T or F) to *both* the negative belief and its fair-pair positive belief, you should consider these *contradictory responses*. An example of contradictory responses is when the student answers "true" to both "I hate school" and "I like school." Because these responses contradict each other, you should not count either one in your scoring. You might sit down with the student and discuss why the student responded the way he or she did and if he or she wouldn't try responding to these items again. If the student has a number of contradictory responses, you might point these out and have him or her take the assessment over again.

Neutral statements have been added as distractors or filler items and are neither compatible nor incompatible with the maladaptive or target behavior. They are not listed in the answer key and do not figure in the scoring. Use the sample assessment and scoring key on the following pages (see Figure A.1) as a guide.

Name _James Jones_____ Date _11/22/98_____

DIRECTIONS: Answer true (T) or false (F). Your answers won't get you into any trouble, so answer the way you really believe.

__T__ 1. If you try, you can change the way you are.

__F__ 2. School is OK.

__F__ 3. Kids who pick on other kids are rotten and deserve to be hurt.

__F__ 4. The worst thing that can happen to you is being teased (picked on) by others (other kids).

__F__ 5. What others think or say about me matters more than what I think about myself.

__T__ 6. It's OK to fight as long as someone else starts it.

__F__ 7. Kids can't hurt me by calling me names.

__F__ 8. School is not as important as people think.

__F__ 9. It's not worth getting into trouble by fighting if somebody picks on you.

__T__ 10. It's not what others think or say about you that matters, it's what you think about yourself that's important.

__T__ 11. Letting someone get away with calling you a name is much worse than anything the teacher or school could do to you.

__F__ 12. I don't want to fight but, the other kids make me by picking on me.

__F__ 13. People (kids) are the way they are and there is nothing they can do about it.

__F__ 14. Kids who fight are tougher than kids who don't.

__F__ 15. School is dumb.

__F__ 16. Fighting only makes things worse.

__T__ 17. It's important to go to school to get an education.

__T__ 18. If you hurt someone who picks on you, he'll leave you alone.

__F__ 19. Sometimes it takes more courage to walk away from a fight than to get into a fight.

__T__ 20. Other kids can't make me do things I don't want to.

__F__ 21. Two wrongs don't make a right. Just because people bug you doesn't mean it's OK to fight them.

__F__ 22. Fighting in school is OK as long as you don't get caught.

__T__ 23. Kids who pick on other kids need to learn how to get along with others.

__T__ 24. Fighting in school should not be allowed.

Figure A.1. Sample completed beliefs assessment.

AGG/PROV

Answer Key

1. The desired responses are listed below. Ideally, the student should answer "false" (F) to items 3, 4, 5, 6, 11, 12, 13, 14, 18, and 22 because they are irrational beliefs (iBs) that are incompatible with the target behavior. Items 1, 7, 9, 10, 16, 19, 20, 21, 23 and 24 should be answered "true" (T) because they are rational beliefs (rBs) that are compatible with the target behavior. Items 2, 8, 15, and 17 are neutral because they have little to do with the target behavior.

2. Use the completed assessment form to write the student's response (T or F) next to each of the desired responses below. For example, if the student's response for #1 is true, record a T next to #1 below.

3. All of the student's responses to the items listed below in the iB column should be false (F). Any response in the iB column answered true (T) should be circled as undesirable. Conversely, all of the student's responses to the items listed below in the rB column should be true (T). Any response in the rB column answered false (F) should be circled as undesirable.

4. A contradictory response occurs when both the iB and its fair-pair rB are answered the same. For example, if the student's responses to #13 and #1 are both false (or both true), this should be considered a contradictory response. Write a question mark (?) next to all contradictory responses.

5. Being careful not to include any contradictory responses, write the number of each iB answered true next to "iB for Disputation" (see below). These are the beliefs the student needs to dispute in order to engage in the target behavior.

Name   James Jones   Date   11/22/98

iB (F)		rB (T)		Neutral (#2, 8, 15, 17)
#13	F	#1	T	
12	F	20	T	
3	F	23	T	**iB for Disputation:**
4	F ?	7	F	#6— "It's OK to fight as long as someone else starts it."
5	F	10	T	
(6)	T	21	F	#11— "Letting someone get away with calling you a name is much worse than anything the teacher or school can do to you."
(11)	T	9	F	
14	F ?	19	F	#18—"If you hurt someone who picks on you, he'll leave you alone."
(18)	T	16	F	
22	F	24	T	

Figure A.1. *Continued.*

Name _____   Date _____

DIRECTIONS: Answer true (T) or false (F). Your answers won't get you into any trouble, so answer the way you really believe.

_____ 1. I like sports.

_____ 2. I feel stupid when I can't do something.

_____ 3. No matter how hard I try, I can't seem to learn new things.

_____ 4. Learning new things is fun.

_____ 5. I shouldn't have to do anything I don't want to.

_____ 6. No matter how hard I try, I can't change the way I am.

_____ 7. When something is hard to do, it is best to give up and not do it.

_____ 8. Nobody can do everything right.

_____ 9. I like school.

_____ 10. I can do anything if I put my mind to it.

_____ 11. Everyone makes mistakes.

_____ 12. I hate schoolwork.

_____ 13. I don't expect to do well in school, so why bother?

_____ 14. Most of the stuff I'm expected to learn in school is not that important.

_____ 15. Everybody has to follow the rules sometimes.

_____ 16. If I don't do my work, I won't learn anything.

_____ 17. It is scary to try new things.

_____ 18. With enough effort, you can change the way you are.

_____ 19. If at first you don't succeed, try, try again.

_____ 20. I can't stand it when I make mistakes.

_____ 21. I have lots of friends.

_____ 22. I like most of my schoolwork.

_____ 23. It is important to get an education.

_____ 24. Everyone should learn how to read, write, and do arithmetic.

_____ 25. If I don't do my work, my teacher(s) will stop giving me work to do.

_____ 26. Most of my schoolwork is fun to do.

Answer Key

1. The desired responses are listed below. Ideally, the student should answer "false"(F) to items 2, 3, 5, 6, 7, 12, 13, 14, 17, 20, and 25 because they are irrational beliefs (iBs) that are incompatible with the target behavior. Items 4, 8, 10, 11, 15, 16, 18, 19, 22, 23, and 24 should be answered "true" (T) because they are rational beliefs (rBs) that are compatible with the target behavior. Items 1, 9, and 21 are neutral because they have little to do with the target behavior.

2. Use the completed assessment form to write the student's response (T or F) next to each of the desired responses below. For example, if the student's response for #2 is false, record an F next to #2 below.

3. All of the student's responses to the items listed below in the iB column should be false (F). Any response in the iB column answered true (T) should be circled as undesirable. Conversely, all of the responses to the items listed below in the rB column should be true (T). Any response in the rB column answered false (F) should be circled as undesirable.

4. A contradictory response occurs when both the iB and its fair-pair rB are answered the same. For example, if the student's responses to #2 and #8 are both false (or both true), this should be considered a contradictory response. Write a question mark (?) next to all contradictory responses.

5. Being careful not to include any contradictory responses, write the number of each iB answered true next to "iB for Disputation" (see below). These are the beliefs the student needs to dispute in order to engage in the target behavior.

Name _____   Date _____

iB (F)	rB (T)	Neutral (#1, 9, 21)
#2	#8	
3	10	
17	4	
5	15	**iB for Disputation:**
6	18	
7	19	
20	11	
12	22	
13	23	
14	24	
25	16	

Name _____ Date _____

DIRECTIONS: Answer true (T) or false (F). Your answers won't get you into any trouble, so answer the way you really believe.

_____ 1. It is important to get an education.

_____ 2. School is OK.

_____ 3. It is OK to run inside the school (classroom) if you are in a hurry.

_____ 4. Sometimes you just have to wait your turn.

_____ 5. Most of the rules at school are dumb.

_____ 6. The only way to get any attention at school is to make your teacher(s) upset.

_____ 7. The work my teacher(s) gives me is boring.

_____ 8. The students who have the fewest friends in school are the ones who get into the most trouble.

_____ 9. I have worth as a person even when others don't pay any attention to me.

_____ 10. I have lots of friends.

_____ 11. I shouldn't have to do anything I don't want to.

_____ 12. With a little effort you can change the way you are.

_____ 13. It's not fair that I can't always be with my friends at school.

_____ 14. The rules at my school are OK.

_____ 15. My worth as a person depends on how much others pay attention to me.

_____ 16. Getting into trouble at school makes you popular with the other students.

_____ 17. I can't help the way I am.

_____ 18. I hate school.

_____ 19. I like sports.

_____ 20. You can't always get what you want when you want it.

_____ 21. Running inside a school building is not safe.

_____ 22. I have to be first all the time.

_____ 23. There are better ways to get attention at school than to make your teacher(s) upset.

_____ 24. Life isn't always fair.

_____ 25. I shouldn't have to wait for anything I want.

_____ 26. Everybody has to follow some rules sometimes.

_____ 27. Most of my schoolwork is fun to do.

INAPP/MOVE

Answer Key

1. The desired responses are listed below. Ideally, the student should answer "false" (F) to items 3, 5, 6, 7, 11, 13, 15, 16, 17, 18, 22, and 25 because they are irrational beliefs (iBs) that are incompatible with the target behavior. Items 2, 4, 8, 9, 12, 14, 20, 21, 23, 24, 26, and 27 should be answered "true" (T) because they are rational beliefs (rBs) that are compatible with the target behavior. Items 1, 10, and 19 are neutral because they have little to do with the target behavior.

2. Use the completed assessment form to write the student's response (T or F) next to each of the desired responses below. For example, if the student's response for #2 is true, record a T next to #2 below.

3. All of the student's responses to the items listed below in the iB column should be false (F). Any response in the iB column answered true (T) should be circled as undesirable. Conversely, all of the student's responses to the items listed below in the rB column should be true (T). Any response in the rB column answered false (F) should be circled as undesirable.

4. A contradictory response occurs when both the iB and its fair-pair rB are answered the same. For example, if the student's responses to #2 and #18 are both false (or both true), this should be considered a contradictory response. Write a question mark (?) next to all contradictory responses.

5. Being careful not to include any contradictory responses, write the number of each iB answered true next to "iB for Disputation" (see below). These are the beliefs the student needs to dispute in order to engage in the target behavior.

Name _____   Date _____

iB (F)	rB (T)	Neutral (#1, 10, 19)
#18	#2	
3	21	
22	4	
5	14	**iB for Disputation:**
6	23	
7	27	
16	8	
15	9	
11	26	
17	12	
13	24	
25	20	

Name _____ Date _____

DIRECTIONS: Answer true (T) or false (F). Your answers won't get you into any trouble, so answer the way you really believe.

_____ 1. People should be able to do whatever they want.

_____ 2. I have lots of friends at school.

_____ 3. It's mean the way teachers (adults) are always trying to control us (students, kids).

_____ 4. It's scary to try new things.

_____ 5. If you try hard enough, you can change the way you are.

_____ 6. The rules at my school are OK.

_____ 7. I'm too old to be told what to do.

_____ 8. Teachers only want you to do what's good for them (like shut up and be good).

_____ 9. I can usually do most of the work at school.

_____ 10. I like sports.

_____ 11. You can learn from your mistakes.

_____ 12. Teachers don't have the right to tell you what to do. Only your parents can do that.

_____ 13. The rules at my school are stupid (unfair).

_____ 14. If students did whatever they wanted at school, nobody would learn anything and people could get hurt.

_____ 15. I hate my teacher(s).

_____ 16. School is dumb.

_____ 17. My teacher usually wants me to do what is best for me (like listen so I can learn).

_____ 18. Most of my teachers are OK.

_____ 19. I hate school.

_____ 20. There shouldn't be any rules at school.

_____ 21. It's a teacher's job to manage students.

_____ 22. By law, teachers are like your parents when you're in school.

_____ 23. No matter how old you get, there are always going to be rules to follow.

_____ 24. No matter how hard you try, you can't change the way you are.

_____ 25. The work at school is too hard for me.

_____ 26. It's important to get an education.

_____ 27. School is OK.

_____ 28. Everybody has to follow rules sometimes.

NONCOMP

Answer Key

1. The desired responses are listed below. Ideally, the student should answer "false"(F) to items 1, 3, 4, 7, 8, 12, 13, 15, 16, 19, 20, 24, and 25 because they are irrational beliefs (iBs) that are incompatible with the target behavior. Items 5, 6, 9, 11, 14, 17, 18, 21, 22, 23, 26, 27, and 28 should be answered "true"(T) because they are rational beliefs (rBs) that are compatible with the target behavior. Items 2 and 10 are neutral items; they have little to do with the target behavior.

2. Use the completed assessment form to write the student's response (T or F) next to each of the desired responses below. For example, if the student's response for #1 is false, record an F next to #1 below.

3. All of the student's responses to the items listed below in the iB column should be false (F). Any response in the iB column answered true (T) should be circled as undesirable. Conversely, all of the student's responses to the items listed below in the rB column should be true (T). Any response in the rB column answered false (F) should be circled as undesirable.

4. A contradictory response occurs when both the iB and its fair-pair rB are answered the same. For example, if the student's responses to #1 and #28 are both false (or both true), this should be considered a contradictory response. Write a question mark (?) next to all contradictory responses.

5. Being careful not to include any contradictory responses, write the number of each iB answered true next to "iB for Disputation" (see below). These are the beliefs the student needs to dispute in order to engage in the target behavior.

Name _____   Date _____

iB (F)	rB (T)	Neutral (#2, 10)
#1	#28	
3	21	
4	11	
7	23	**iB for Disputation:**
12	22	
13	6	
20	14	
19	27	
15	18	
8	17	
25	9	
24	5	
16	26	

DIST/ATT SEEK

Name _____ Date _____

DIRECTIONS: Answer true (T) or false (F). Your answers won't get you into any trouble, so answer the way you really believe.

_____ 1. I have lots of friends.

_____ 2. School can be fun when you do your work and learn new things.

_____ 3. It's not fair when others get more attention than I do.

_____ 4. I can't help the way I am.

_____ 5. I would probably get more attention at school by behaving myself.

_____ 6. No matter what the consequences are, I must be noticed or else I am lost and worthless.

_____ 7. Students who get into trouble at school have fewer friends than students who are good.

_____ 8. I am disappointed when I don't get called on but there is always next time.

_____ 9. I shouldn't have to wait for anything I want.

_____ 10. I can't stand it when people ignore me.

_____ 11. Getting into trouble at school is a good way to make friends.

_____ 12. The only way I can get any attention at school is to get into trouble.

_____ 13. One has to accept the fact that some things in life are just not fair.

_____ 14. With a little effort, you can change your behavior.

_____ 15. What I think about myself is more important than what others think about me.

_____ 16. It is important to get an education.

_____ 17. I'd rather be ignored by someone than have him (her) mad at me.

_____ 18. You can't always get what you want when you want it.

_____ 19. I can't stand it when I raise my hand and the teacher ignores me.

_____ 20. I like school.

_____ 21. I have worth as a person even when others don't pay attention to me.

_____ 22. I like sports.

_____ 23. What others think about me is more important than what I think about myself.

DIST/ATT SEEK

Answer Key

1. The desired responses are listed below. Ideally, the student should answer "false" (F) to items 3, 4, 6, 9, 10, 11, 12, 19, and 23 because they are irrational beliefs (iBs) that are incompatible with the target behavior. Items 5, 7, 8, 13, 14, 15, 17, 18, and 21 should be answered "true" (T) because they are rational beliefs (rBs) that are compatible with the target behavior. Items 1, 2, 16, 20, and 22 are neutral because they have little to do with the target behavior.

2. Use the completed assessment form to write the student's response (T or F) next to each of the desired responses below. For example, if the student's response for #3 is false, record an F next to #3 below.

3. All of the student's responses to the items listed below in the iB column should be false (F). Any response in the iB column answered true (T) should be circled as undesirable. Conversely, all of the student's responses to the items listed below in the rB column should be true (T). Any response in the rB column answered false (F) should be circled as undesirable.

4. A contradictory response occurs when both the iB and its fair-pair rB are answered the same. For example, if the student's responses to #3 and #13 are both false (or both true), this should be considered a contradictory response. Write a question mark (?) next to all contradictory responses.

5. Being careful not to include any contradictory responses, write the number of each iB answered true next to "iB for Disputation" (see below). These are the beliefs the student needs to dispute in order to engage in the target behavior.

Name _____   Date _____

iB (F)	rB (T)	Neutral (#1, 2, 16, 20, 22)
#3	#13	
4	14	
12	5	
6	21	**iB for Disputation:**
11	7	
19	8	
9	18	
10	17	
23	15	

Name _____ Date _____

DIRECTIONS: Answer true (T) or false (T). Your answers won't get you into any trouble, so answer the way you really believe.

_____ 1. It's not fair when things don't go my way.

_____ 2. I have lots of friends.

_____ 3. When things don't go my way, it's awful and I can't stand it.

_____ 4. You can't always get what you want.

_____ 5. It's OK to make mistakes.

_____ 6. People must do what I want them to.

_____ 7. I shouldn't have to wait for anything I want.

_____ 8. Life isn't always fair.

_____ 9. When I want something badly enough, I must get it.

_____ 10. School is hard.

_____ 11. It's disappointing when things don't go my way, but it's not the end of the world.

_____ 12. If people don't do what I want them to, it means they don't like me.

_____ 13. I should get whatever I want whenever I want it.

_____ 14. Wanting something badly doesn't entitle you to it.

_____ 15. Nobody likes me.

_____ 16. It's possible that people who like me might not do what I want them to.

_____ 17. People who don't do what I want are bad and should be punished.

_____ 18. If you try, you can change the way you are.

_____ 19. I'm a pretty good person.

_____ 20. Waiting for things can help you learn patience.

_____ 21. I can't expect everybody to do what I tell them to.

_____ 22. A person can still be good even though he or she doesn't do what I want.

_____ 23. People are the way they are and there is nothing they can do about it.

_____ 24. If at first you don't succeed, try, try again.

TANT/REFUS

Answer Key

1. The desired responses are listed below. Ideally, the student should answer "false" (F) to items 1, 3, 6, 7, 9, 12, 13, 17, and 23 because they are irrational beliefs (iBs) that are incompatible with the target behavior. Items 4, 8, 11, 14, 16, 18, 20, 21, and 22 should be answered "true" (T) because they are rational beliefs (rBs) that are compatible with the target behavior. Items 2, 5, 10, 15, 19, and 24 are neutral because they have little to do with the target behavior.

2. Use the completed assessment form to write the student's response (T or F) next to each of the desired responses below. For example, if the student's response for #1 is true, record a T next to #1 below.

3. All of the student's responses to the items listed below in the iB column should be false (F). Any response in the iB column answered true (T) should be circled as undesirable. Conversely, all of the student's responses to the items listed below in the rB column should be true (T). Any response in the rB column answered false (F) should be circled as undesirable.

4. A contradictory response occurs when the responses to both the iB and its fair-pair rB are answered the same. For example, if the student's responses to #1 and #8 are both false (or both true), this should be considered a contradictory response. Write a question mark (?) next to all contradictory responses.

5. Being careful not to include any contradictory responses, write the number of each iB answered true next to "iB for Disputation" (see below). These are the beliefs the student needs to dispute in order to engage in the target behavior.

Name _____   Date _____

iB (F)	rB (T)	Neutral (#2, 5, 10, 15, 19, 24)
#1	#8	
3	11	
13	4	
7	20	**iB for Disputation:**
6	21	
9	14	
12	16	
17	22	
23	18	

EXTORT

Name _____ Date _____

DIRECTIONS: Answer true (T) or false (F). Your answers won't get you into any trouble, so answer the way you really believe.

_____ 1. I can always learn from my mistakes.

_____ 2. It is important to get an education.

_____ 3. I should always get what I want.

_____ 4. I can't help the way I am.

_____ 5. Most of the kids at school don't like me anyway, so why try to be nice to them.

_____ 6. My schoolmates are punks.

_____ 7. You should treat others the same way you want to be treated.

_____ 8. Being nice to others makes you look weak.

_____ 9. When you want something badly, it doesn't matter what you do to get it.

_____ 10. I should not expect everybody to obey me.

_____ 11. I'd rather be liked by others than feared by them.

_____ 12. With a little effort, you can change your behavior.

_____ 13. Whether people like you or not depends on how you treat them.

_____ 14. If people don't do what I want, it means they are bad and should be punished.

_____ 15. You can't always get what you want.

_____ 16. I like most of my schoolmates.

_____ 17. Being nice to others is its own reward.

_____ 18. School is hard.

_____ 19. People are supposed to do what I want.

_____ 20. People are either going to like you or they're not; there isn't much you can do about it.

_____ 21. Once the kids at school get to know me, they like me.

_____ 22. It doesn't matter whether people like you or not, as long as they do what you want.

_____ 23. I like school.

_____ 24. Wanting something never gives you the right to treat others badly.

EXTORT

Answer Key

1. The desired responses are listed below. Ideally, the student should answer "false" (F) to items 3, 4, 5, 6, 8, 9, 14, 19, 20 and 22 because they are irrational beliefs (iBs) that are incompatible with the target behavior. Items 7, 10, 11, 12, 13, 15, 16, 17, 21, and 24 should be answered "true" (T) because they are rational beliefs (rBs) that are compatible with the target behavior. Items 1, 2, 18, and 23 are neutral because they have little to do with the target behavior.

2. Use the completed assessment form to write the student's response (T or F) next to each of the desired responses below. For example, if the student's response for #3 is false, record an F next to #3 below.

3. All of the student's responses to the items listed below in the iB column should be false (F). Any response in the iB column answered true (T) should be circled as undesirable. Conversely, all of the student's responses to the items listed below in the rB column should be true (T). Any response in the rB column answered false (F) should be circled as undesirable.

4. A contradictory response occurs when both the iB and its fair-pair rB are answered the same. For example, if the student's responses to #3 and #15 are both false (or both true), this should be considered a contradictory response. Write a question mark (?) next to all contradictory responses.

5. Being careful not to include any contradictory responses, write the number of each iB answered true next to "iB for Disputation" (see below). These are the beliefs the student needs to dispute in order to engage in the target behavior.

Name _____   Date _____

iB (F)	rB (T)	Neutral (1, 2, 18, 23)
#3	#15	
9	24	
19	10	
4	12	**iB for Disputation:**
20	13	
5	21	
6	16	
14	7	
8	17	
22	11	

DEST PROP

Name _____ Date _____

DIRECTIONS: Answer true (T) or false (F). Your answers won't get you into any trouble, so answer the way you really believe.

_____ 1. It's not fair when things don't go my way.

_____ 2. I like school.

_____ 3. With a little effort, you can change the way you are.

_____ 4. If I can't get what I want, nobody should.

_____ 5. When things don't go my way, it's awful and I can't stand it.

_____ 6. Making mistakes is awful.

_____ 7. You can't always get what you want.

_____ 8. It's OK to make mistakes.

_____ 9. It's important to get an education.

_____ 10. Life isn't always fair.

_____ 11. Sometimes the only way to get any attention is to upset others.

_____ 12. Once people get to know me, they like me.

_____ 13. You can show respect for others by respecting their property.

_____ 14. People who don't do what I want are bad and should be punished.

_____ 15. I should be disappointed when I don't get what I want and happy for others when they do.

_____ 16. Nobody likes me.

_____ 17. School is hard.

_____ 18. No matter how hard I try, I can't change the way I am.

_____ 19. I should get whatever I want whenever I want it.

_____ 20. There are better ways to get attention than to upset others.

_____ 21. You should treat others the way you want to be treated.

_____ 22. Nobody respects my rights, so why should I respect theirs?

_____ 23. I hate school.

_____ 24. It's disappointing when things don't go my way, but it's not the end of the world.

DEST PROP

Answer Key

1. The desired responses are listed below. Ideally, the student should answer "false" (F) to items 1, 4, 5, 6, 11, 14, 16, 18, 19, and 22 because they are irrational beliefs (iBs) that are incompatible with the target behavior. Items 3, 7, 8, 10, 12, 13, 15, 20, 21, and 24 should be answered "true" (T) because they are rational beliefs (rBs) that are compatible with the target behavior. Items 2, 9, 17, and 23 are neutral because they have little to do with the target behavior.

2. Use the completed assessment form to write the student's response (T or F) next to each of the desired responses below. For example, if the student's response for #1 is false, record an F next to #1 below.

3. All of the student's responses to the items listed below in the iB column should be false (F). Any response in the iB column answered true (T) should be circled as undesirable. Conversely, all of the student's responses to the items listed below in the rB column should be true (T). Any response in the rB column answered false (F) should be circled as undesirable.

4. A contradictory response occurs when both the iB and its fair-pair rB are answered the same. For example, if the student's responses to #1 and #10 are both false (or both true), this should be considered a contradictory response. Write a question mark (?) next to all contradictory responses.

5. Being careful not to include any contradictory responses, write the number of each iB answered true next to "iB for Disputation" (see below). These are the beliefs the student needs to dispute in order to engage in the target behavior.

Name _____   Date _____

ib (F)	rB (T)	Neutral (#2, 9, 17, 23)
#1	#10	
18	3	
4	15	
16	12	iB for Disputation:
5	24	
19	7	
6	8	
14	21	
11	20	
22	13	

Name _____ Date _____

DIRECTIONS: Answer true (T) or false (F). Your answers won't get you into any trouble, so answer the way you really believe.

_____ 1. If you try, you can change the way you are.

_____ 2. School is OK.

_____ 3. Kids who pick on other kids are rotten and deserve to be hurt.

_____ 4. The worst thing that can happen to you is being teased (picked on) by others (other kids).

_____ 5. What others think or say about me matters more than what I think about myself.

_____ 6. It's OK to fight as long as someone else starts it.

_____ 7. Kids can't hurt me by calling me names.

_____ 8. School is not as important as people think.

_____ 9. It's not worth getting into trouble by fighting if somebody picks on you.

_____ 10. It's not what others think or say about you that matters, it's what you think about yourself that's important.

_____ 11. Letting someone get away with calling you a name is much worse than anything the teacher or school could do to you.

_____ 12. I don't want to fight, but the other kids make me by picking on me.

_____ 13. People (kids) are the way they are and there is nothing they can do about it.

_____ 14. Kids who fight are tougher than kids who don't.

_____ 15. School is dumb.

_____ 16. Fighting only makes things worse.

_____ 17. It's important to go to school to get an education.

_____ 18. If you hurt someone who picks on you, he'll leave you alone.

_____ 19. Sometimes it takes more courage to walk away from a fight than to get into a fight.

_____ 20. Other kids can't make me do things I don't want to.

_____ 21. Two wrongs don't make a right. Just because people bug you doesn't mean it's OK to fight them.

_____ 22. Fighting in school is OK as long as you don't get caught.

_____ 23. Kids who pick on other kids need to learn how to get along with others.

_____ 24. Fighting in school should not be allowed.

Answer Key

1. The desired responses are listed below. Ideally, the student should answer "false" (F) to items 3, 4, 5, 6, 11, 12, 13, 14, 18, and 22 because they are irrational beliefs (iBs) that are incompatible with the target behavior. Items 1, 7, 9, 10, 16, 19, 20, 21, 23 and 24 should be answered "true" (T) because they are rational beliefs (rBs) that are compatible with the target behavior. Items 2, 8, 15, and 17 are neutral because they have little to do with the target behavior.

2. Use the completed assessment form to write the student's response (T or F) next to each of the desired responses below. For example, if the student's response for #1 is true, record a T next to #1 below.

3. All of the student's responses to the items listed below in the iB column should be false (F). Any response in the iB column answered true (T) should be circled as undesirable. Conversely, all of the student's responses to the items listed below in the rB column should be true (T). Any response in the rB column answered false (F) should be circled as undesirable.

4. A contradictory response occurs when both the iB and its fair-pair rB are answered the same. For example, if the student's responses to #13 and #1 are both false (or both true), this should be considered a contradictory response. Write a question mark (?) next to all contradictory responses.

5. Being careful not to include any contradictory responses, write the number of each iB answered true next to "iB for Disputation" (see below). These are the beliefs the student needs to dispute in order to engage in the target behavior.

Name _____   Date _____

iB (F)	rB (T)	Neutral (#2, 8, 15, 17)
#13	#1	
12	20	
3	23	**iB for Disputation:**
4	7	
5	10	
6	21	
11	9	
14	19	
18	16	
22	24	

Name _____ Date _____

DIRECTIONS: Answer true (T) or false (F). Your answers won't get you into any trouble, so answer the way you really believe.

_____ 1. I like school.

_____ 2. You can always learn from your mistakes.

_____ 3. You should treat others the way you want to be treated.

_____ 4. I don't like most of my classmates.

_____ 5. Most of the students (kids) at school don't like me anyway, so why should I try to be nice to them?

_____ 6. People make me angry.

_____ 7. It doesn't make any difference whether others like me or not.

_____ 8. It is important to get an education.

_____ 9. Most of the time I would rather be liked than disliked.

_____ 10. Being nice to others is its own reward.

_____ 11. Others can't make you angry. Only you can make yourself angry.

_____ 12. There are better ways to get attention than to get others upset at you.

_____ 13. I can't help the way I act around others. That's just the way I am.

_____ 14. Being nice to others is a sign of weakness.

_____ 15. I hate school.

_____ 16. Once the kids at school get to know me, they like me.

_____ 17. With a little effort, you can change your behavior.

_____ 18. Teasing is harmless fun.

_____ 19. Most people I know are rotten and deserve to be treated badly.

_____ 20. People will either like you or they won't. There isn't much you can do about it.

_____ 21. Making people angry or upset can sometimes get you hurt.

_____ 22. Most of my classmates are OK.

_____ 23. Sometimes the only way to get any attention is to upset people.

_____ 24. Whether or not people like you depends on how you treat them.

VERB AGG/NO PROV

Answer Key

1. The desired responses are listed below. Ideally, the student should answer "false" (F) to items 4, 5, 6, 7, 13, 14, 18, 19, 20, and 23 because they are irrational beliefs (iBs) that are incompatible with the target behavior. Items 3, 9, 10, 11, 12, 16, 17, 21, 22, and 24 should be answered "true" (T) because they are rational beliefs (rBs) that are compatible with the target behavior. Items 1, 2, 8, and 15 are neutral because they have little to do with the target behavior.

2. Use the completed assessment form to write the student's response (T or F) next to each of the desired responses below. For example, if the student's response for #3 is true, record a T next to #3 below.

3. All of the student's responses to the items listed below in the iB column should be false (F). Any response in the iB column answered true (T) should be circled as undesirable. Conversely, all of the student's responses to the items listed below in the rB column should be true (T). Any response in the rB column answered false (F) should be circled as undesirable.

4. A contradictory response occurs when both the iB and its fair-pair rB are answered the same. For example, if the student's responses to #3 and #19 are both false (or both true), this should be considered a contradictory response. Write a question mark (?) next to all contradictory responses.

5. Being careful not to include any contradictory responses, write the number of each iB answered true next to "iB for Disputation" (see below). These are the beliefs the student needs to dispute in order to engage in the target behavior.

Name _____   Date _____

ib (F)	rB (T)	Neutral (#1, 2, 8, 15)
#19	#3	
4	22	
5	16	
6	11	**iB for Disputation:**
7	9	
18	21	
14	10	
13	17	
20	24	
23	12	

PHYS AGG/NO PROV

Name _____ Date _____

DIRECTIONS: Answer true (T) or false (F). Your answers won't get you into any trouble, so answer the way you really believe.

_____ 1. You can always learn from your mistakes.

_____ 2. You should treat others the way you want to be treated.

_____ 3. People make me angry.

_____ 4. It doesn't make any difference whether others like me or not.

_____ 5. I can't help the way I act around others. That's just the way I am.

_____ 6. It is always better to be feared than liked.

_____ 7. It is important to get an education.

_____ 8. With a little effort, you can change your behavior.

_____ 9. People who treat others nicely usually get treated nicely in return.

_____ 10. Most people I know are rotten and deserve to be treated badly.

_____ 11. Whether or not people like you depends on how you treat them.

_____ 12. School is hard.

_____ 13. I like most of my classmates.

_____ 14. Others can't make you angry. Only you can make yourself angry.

_____ 15. Being nice makes you look weak.

_____ 16. Most of the time I would rather be liked than disliked.

_____ 17. I like sports.

_____ 18. I would rather be liked than feared.

_____ 19. I don't like most of my classmates.

_____ 20. People will either like you or they won't. There isn't much you can do about it.

_____ 21. Being nice to others is its own reward.

_____ 22. Once the kids at school get to know me, they like me.

_____ 23. Being nice to others is a sign of weakness.

_____ 24. Most of the students (kids) at school don't like me anyway, so why should I try to be nice to them?

PHYS AGG/NO PROV

Answer Key

1. The desired responses are listed below. Ideally, the student should answer "false" (F) to items 3, 4, 5, 6, 10, 15, 19, 20, 23, and 24 because they are irrational beliefs (iBs) that are incompatible with the target behavior. Items 2, 8, 9, 11, 13, 14, 16, 18, 21, and 22 should be answered "true" (T) because they are rational beliefs (rBs) that are compatible with the target behavior. Items 1, 7, 12, and 17 are neutral because they have little to do with the target behavior.

2. Use the completed assessment form to write the student's response (T or F) next to each of the desired responses below. For example, if the student's response for #2 is true, record a T next to #2 below.

3. All of the student's responses to the items listed below in the iB column should be false (F). Any response in the iB column answered true (T) should be circled as undesirable. Conversely, all of the student's responses to the items listed below in the rB column should be true (T). Any response in the rB column answered false (F) should be circled as undesirable.

4. A contradictory response occurs when both the iB and its fair-pair rB are answered the same. For example, if the student's responses to #2 and #10 are both false (or both true), this should be considered a contradictory response. Write a question mark (?) next to all contradictory responses.

5. Being careful not to include any contradictory responses, write the number of each iB answered true next to "iB for Disputation" (see below). These are the beliefs the student needs to dispute in order to engage in the target behavior.

Name _____   Date _____

ib (F)	rB (T)	Neutral (#1, 7, 12, 17)
#10	#2	
3	14	
4	16	
5	8	**iB for Disputation:**
6	18	
15	9	
20	11	
19	13	
23	21	
24	22	

Performance Objectives

The performance objectives on the following pages may be used in student IEPs and BIPs. Each objective tells you the behavior the student must perform, the conditions under which he or she must perform it, and how well he or she must perform it (criteria for acceptable performance, or CAP) *to demonstrate that he or she has the prerequisite in question.* Think of the objective as the destination in a trip and the intervention as the vehicle or means of getting there. The objective tells you when your student has arrived at the destination so that you can stop using your intervention.

1.0 *Target Behavior:* Student works on assigned tasks with minimal or no supervision.

1.1 *Expectation:* When asked what he or she is supposed to do when given a task (work) to do in class, the student will answer correctly with little or no prompting within 10 seconds of being asked. To be correct, the student's response must convey the idea that he or she is expected to work on the task without prompting (reminders) from the teacher.

1.2 *Awareness:* When the teacher and the target student each monitor the student's on-task behavior (i.e., head oriented toward work) on three separate trials, there will be at least 80% (cumulative) interobserver agreement.

1.3 *Self-Control:* When the teacher monitors the level of affect (LOA) in the target student and a small sample of peers, some with and some without signs of depression, on three separate trials, the target student's data (i.e., median LOA) will more closely resemble the data (median LOA) from the nondepressed sample than the data of the depressed sample.

1.4 *Competence:* Given a curriculum-based assessment to assess his or her competence at performing assigned academic tasks, the student will meet the CAP for all assigned tasks.

1.5 *Motivation:* Given all of the consequences of working independently and working only when supervised, the student will identify all of the consequences of working independently as those he or she likes and the consequences of working only when supervised as those he or she dislikes.

1.6 *Beliefs:* Given a beliefs assessment, the student will identify all beliefs compatible with working independently as true and all beliefs incompatible with working independently as false. He or she will do this on at least two consecutive administrations with a 24-hour latency between assessments.

2.0 *Target Behavior:* Student engages in physical activity (movement) in school that is appropriate according to frequency, situation, and setting.

2.1 *Expectation:* When asked how he or she is supposed to use his or her body (i.e., run, walk, sit, stand, jump) in a variety of school settings (e.g., classroom, halls, playground, cafeteria, gym) and situations (e.g., free time, independent seatwork, class lessons, moving between classrooms, lunch, recess, assemblies), the student will answer correctly with little or no prompting within 10 seconds of being asked *for each example.* To be correct, the student's responses must convey the idea that he or she knows that he or she is expected to sit and walk in all school settings except for the playground and the gym.

2.2 *Awareness:* When the teacher and the target student each monitor the student's inappropriate movement *in the classroom* on three separate trials, there will be at least 80% (cumulative) interobserver agreement. Appropriate movement in the classroom includes sitting, standing, or walking when acceptable to do so. Inappropriate movement includes running, jumping up and down, and other excessive movement when it is not acceptable to do so.

2.3 *Self-Control:* When the teacher monitors the frequency of observable signs of anxiety in the target student and in a small sample of peers, some with and some without signs of anxiety, on three separate trials, the target student's data (i.e., median score of three trials) will more closely resemble the data (median score of three trials) from the nonanxious sample than the data of the anxious sample. The same objective will be met for the frequency of impulsivity in the target student.

2.4 *Competence:* When cued to do so, the student will demonstrate the competencies of staying in his or her seat for a period of time, walking around the classroom, and walking in the hallway. He or she will perform each competency in a manner judged acceptable by the teacher.

2.5 *Motivation:* Given the consequences of appropriate movement (i.e., sitting, standing, walking) in the classroom and the hall and the consequences of inappropriate movement (i.e., running in class or hall, jumping up and down in class), the student will identify all consequences of appropriate movement as those he or she likes and all consequences of inappropriate movement as those he or she dislikes.

2.6 *Beliefs:* Given a beliefs assessment, the student will identify all beliefs compatible with appropriate movement in school as true and all beliefs incompatible with appropriate movement in school as false. He or she will do this on at least two consecutive administrations with a 24-hour latency between assessments.

3.0 *Target Behavior:* Student will follow all reasonable and fair directives that all students are expected to follow at school. He or she will follow them the first time given and in a manner deemed acceptable by the person giving the directive.

3.1 *Expectation:* When asked what he or she is supposed to do when a teacher, staff member, or administrator asks him or her to do something that all students are expected to do at school, the student will answer correctly with little or no prompting within 10 seconds of being asked. To be correct, the student's response must convey the idea that he or she knows that he or she is expected to comply with a directive the first time it is given and in a manner deemed acceptable by the person giving the directive.

3.2 *Awareness:* When the teacher and the target student each monitor his or her compliant and noncompliant behavior on three separate trials, there will be at least 80% (cumulative) interobserver agreement.

3.3 *Self-Control:* When the teacher monitors the frequency of observable signs of anxiety in the target student and a small sample of peers, some with and some without signs of anxiety, on three separate trials, the target student's data (i.e., median score of three trials) will more closely resemble the data (median score of three trials) from the nonanxious sample than the data from the anxious sample.

3.4 *Competence:* Given a curriculum-based assessment to assess his or her competence at performing various directives given at school, the student will meet the CAP for all directives given.

3.5 *Motivation:* Given all of the consequences of compliance and of noncompliance, the student will identify all consequences of compliance as those he or she likes and all consequences of noncompliance as those he or she dislikes.

3.6 *Beliefs:* Given a beliefs assessment, the student will identify all beliefs compatible with compliance as true and all beliefs incompatible with compliance as false. He or she will do this on at least two consecutive administrations with a 24-hour latency between assessments.

4.0 *Target Behavior:* Student will seek attention from peers or adults during academic instruction time in a nondisruptive manner (e.g., raise hand and wait, speak quietly, make eye contact, stay in one place).

4.1 *Expectation:* When asked what he or she is supposed to do when he or she wants attention from the teacher or peers in the classroom, the student will answer correctly with little or no prompting within 10 seconds of being asked. To be correct, the student's response must convey the idea that he or she knows that he or she is expected to use nondisruptive means (e.g., raise hand and wait, speak quietly, make eye contact, stay in one place) to gain attention.

4.2 *Awareness:* When the teacher and the target student each monitor the student's nondisruptive and disruptive attention-seeking behavior on three separate trials, there will be at least 80% (cumulative) interobserver agreement.

4.3 *Self-Control:* When the teacher monitors the frequency of observable signs of anxiety in the target student and in a small sample of peers, some with and some without signs of anxiety, on three separate trials, the target student's data (median score of three trials) will more closely resemble the data (median scores) from the nonanxious sample than the data from the anxious sample over a 3-day period. The same objective will be met for the frequency of impulsivity in the target student.

4.4 *Competence:* When cued to do so, the student will demonstrate appropriate attention-seeking behavior in at least two of three role play situations without any prompting from the teacher. Appropriateness to be judged by the teacher.

4.5 *Motivation:* Given all of the consequences of nondisruptive and disruptive attention seeking, the student will identify all of the consequences for nondisruptive attention seeking as those he or she likes and all of the consequences for disruptive attention seeking as those he or she dislikes.

4.6 *Beliefs:* Given a beliefs assessment, the student will identify all beliefs compatible with nondisruptive attention seeking as true and all beliefs incompatible with nondisruptive attention seeking as false. He or she will do this on at least two consecutive administrations with a 24-hour latency between assessments.

5.0 *Target Behavior:* Student will respond in a socially appropriate manner (i.e., will repeat the request, ask for an explanation, negotiate, or accept the refusal) when his or her requests are not met.

5.1 *Expectation:* When asked what he or she is supposed to do when someone at school does not do what he or she wants, the student will answer correctly with little or no prompting. To be correct, the student's response must convey the idea that he or she knows that he or she is expected to do one or more of the following: repeat the request, ask for an explanation, negotiate, or accept the refusal. The student will do so within 10 seconds of being asked.

5.2 *Awareness:* When the teacher and the target student each monitor the student's appropriate (i.e., repeats request, asks for explanation, negotiates, accepts refusal) and inappropriate (tantrum) responses when his or her requests are not met by a peer or an adult at school, there will be at least 80% interobserver (cumulative) agreement on three separate trials of monitoring.

5.3 *Self-Control:* When the teacher monitors the frequency of obvious signs of anger in the target student and a small sample of peers, some with and some without anger signs, on three separate trials, the target student's data (median score of three trials) will more closely resemble the data (median scores) of the nonangry sample than the data of the angry sample.

5.4 *Competence:* Given a role play situation in which his or her requests are refused, the student will demonstrate socially appropriate responses to each refusal. He or she will repeat the request, ask for an explanation, try to negotiate, or accept the refusal in at least two of the three role plays without any prompting from the teacher.

5.5 *Motivation:* Given all of the consequences of socially appropriate and inappropriate responses to request refusals, the student will identify all of the consequences for socially appropriate responses as those he or she likes and all of the consequences for inappropriate responses as those he or she dislikes.

5.6 *Beliefs:* Given a beliefs assessment, the student will identify all beliefs compatible with socially appropriate responses to request refusals as true and all beliefs

incompatible with such responses as false. He or she will do this on at least two consecutive administrations with a 24-hour latency between assessments.

5.7 *Perception of Solutions:* Given problems involving request refusals, the student will generate at least two acceptable solutions for each of two problems. To be acceptable, each solution must be considered effective (i.e., will get student what he or she wants without creating new problems), feasible (i.e., is something he or she is able and willing to do), and prosocial (i.e., considered acceptable behavior by the school) in the teacher's judgment.

6.0 *Target Behavior:* Student will make requests of others in the form of a question (e.g., "May I . . .") instead of a demand (e.g., "Give me . . .") and, if compliance is delayed or refused, he or she will repeat the request or accept the refusal without threatening aversive consequences.

6.1 *Expectation:* When asked what he or she is supposed to do when he or she wants someone to do something for him or her, the student will answer correctly with little or no prompting within 10 seconds of being asked. To be correct, the student's response must convey the idea that he or she knows that he or she is expected to make his or her request in the form of a question instead of a demand and, if compliance is delayed or refused, he or she is to repeat the request or accept the refusal without threatening aversive consequences.

6.2 *Awareness:* When the teacher and the target student each monitor the student's prosocial (i.e., he or she asks, and if compliance is delayed or refused, he or she asks again or accepts refusal) and antisocial (i.e., he or she demands, and if compliance is delayed or refused, he or she threatens aversive consequences) requests of others, there will be at least 80% (cumulative) interobserver agreement on 2 out of 3 days of monitoring.

6.3 *Self-Control:* When the teacher monitors the frequency of observable signs of anger in the target student and a small sample of peers, some with and some without signs of anger, on three separate trials, the target student's data (median score of three trials) more closely resemble the data (median scores) from the nonangry sample than the data from the angry sample

6.4 *Competence:* Given three role play situations in which the target student attempts to get something from others, he or she will demonstrate prosocial behavior in all three roles. To be considered prosocial, the request must be made in the form of a question instead of a demand, and if compliance is slow, the student will either keep asking or accept the refusal without threatening aversive consequences.

6.5 *Motivation:* Given all of the consequences of attempts to get something from others in a prosocial and antisocial manner, the student will identify all those consequences of prosocial behavior as things that he or she likes and all consequences of antisocial behavior as things he or she dislikes.

6.6 *Beliefs:* Given a beliefs assessment, the student will identify all beliefs compatible with making prosocial requests as true and all beliefs incompatible with making prosocial requests as false. He or she will do so on two consecutive administrations with a 24-hour latency between assessments.

7.0 *Target Behavior:* Student will handle property of others in a nondestructive way (i.e., as it was intended, without trying to harm it).

7.1 *Expectation:* When asked how he or she is expected to handle the property of others, the student will answer correctly with little or no prompting within 10 seconds of being asked. The student's response may be considered correct if it conveys the idea that he or she knows that he or she is expected to handle the property of others the way it was intended and without trying to damage it.

7.2 *Awareness:* After monitoring the frequency (i.e., number of occurrences) of destructive behavior in the target student over a predetermined interval, the teacher will ask the student how many times he or she thinks he or she engaged in destructive behavior. When the teacher's data and the student's data are compared, there should be at least 80% agreement between the two sets of data on two out of three intervals.

7.3 *Self-Control:* When the teacher monitors the frequency of obvious signs of anger in the target student and a small sample of peers, some with anger signs and some without, on three separate trials, the target student's data (median score of three trials) more closely resemble the data (median scores) of peers without anger problems. The same objective will be met by the student for impulsivity.

7.4 *Competence:* Given school property (e.g., books, crayons, pencils, paper, furniture) and personal property of others, the student will demonstrate the correct handling and use of each over a brief period of time. The item will be used as it was intended and will be returned to the owner in the same or similar condition as it was received.

7.5 *Motivation:* Given all of the consequences of handling the property of others in a nondestructive and destructive manner, the student will identify all of the consequences of nondestructive handling as those he or she likes and all of the consequences of destructive handling as those he or she dislikes.

7.6 *Beliefs:* Given a beliefs assessment, the student will identify all beliefs compatible with nondestructive handling of others' property as true and all beliefs incompatible with nondestructive handling of others' property as false. He or she will do this on at least two consecutive administrations with a 24-hour latency between assessments.

8.0 *Target Behavior:* When provoked by peers (i.e., teasing, threats, insulting, swearing, disapproval), the student responds assertively (i.e., tells peers to stop and says what he or she feels about their behavior), without being aggressive.

8.1 *Expectation:* When asked what he or she is expected to do when someone teases him or her (or threatens, calls him or her a name, makes fun of him or her, puts him or her down) at school, the student will answer correctly with little or no prompting within 10 seconds of being asked. To be considered correct the student's response must convey the idea that he or she knows that he or she is expected to respond assertively (i.e., tells them to stop and says how he or she feels) without any aggressive behavior.

8.2 *Awareness:* The teacher will monitor the target student's responses to peer provocations over a predetermined interval and calculate the percentage of aggressive and assertive responses. The teacher will then ask the student how many times he or she was provoked and how many of those times he or she responded in an aggressive way and in an assertive way. When the teacher's data and the student's data are compared, there should be at least 80% agreement between the two sets of data on two out of three intervals.

8.3 *Self-Control:* When the teacher monitors the frequency of obvious signs of anger in the target student and a small sample of peers, some with and some without signs of anger, over three separate trials, the target student's data (median score of three trials) more closely resemble the data (median scores) of peers without anger problems on 2 of the 3 days of monitoring. The same objective will be met for the frequency of impulsivity.

8.4 *Competence:* Given three role play situations involving peer provocation, the student will correctly demonstrate assertive responses in two of the three situations without any prompting. For the response to be considered correct, the student must remain composed (no visible signs of anger or anxiety), make direct eye contact, keep hands at sides, and say, "Don't say (or do) that. I don't like it," using a firm, but conversational, tone of voice without any aggressive behavior (e.g., body posturing, cursing, threats, or physical contact).

8.5 *Motivation:* Given all of the consequences of assertive and aggressive responses to peer provocation, the student will identify all of the consequences of assertive responding as those he or she likes and all of the consequences of aggressive responding as those he or she dislikes.

8.6 *Beliefs:* Given a beliefs assessment, the student will identify all beliefs compatible with assertive responding to peer provocation as true and all beliefs incompatible with assertive responding as false. He or she will do this on at least two consecutive administrations with a 24-hour latency between assessments.

8.7 *Perception of Solutions:* Given problems involving peer provocation, the student will generate at least two acceptable solutions for each of two problems. To be acceptable, the solution must be considered effective (i.e., solve the problem without creating new ones), feasible (i.e., something the student is willing and able to do), and prosocial (i.e., considered acceptable behavior by the school) in the judgment of the teacher.

9.0 *Target Behavior:* The student will interact with peers in a prosocial manner (i.e., making positive or neutral comments without swearing at, insulting, disapproving of, threatening, or teasing).

9.1 *Expectation:* When asked how he or she is supposed to behave when he or she interacts (talks with) his or her peers at school, the student will answer correctly with little or no prompting from the teacher within 10 seconds of being asked. To be considered correct, the student's response must convey the idea that he or she knows that he or she is expected to interact in a prosocial way (i.e., make positive or neutral comments to peers without any teasing, threatening, insulting, swearing at, or disapproving of).

9.2 *Awareness:* After monitoring the frequency (i.e., number of occurrences) of unprovoked verbally aggressive behavior in the target student over a predetermined interval, the teacher will ask the student how many times he or she thinks he or she engaged in this behavior. When the teacher's data and the student's data are compared, there should be at least 80% agreement between the two sets of data on two out of three intervals.

9.3 *Self-Control:* When the teacher monitors the frequency of observable signs of anger in the target student and in a small sample of peers, some with and some without signs of anger, on three separate trials, the target student's data (median score of three trials) will more closely resemble the data from the nonangry sample than the data from the angry sample. The same objective will be met by the student for the frequency of impulsivity.

9.4 *Competence:* Given a standardized social skills assessment with the focus on conversational skills with peers, the student will demonstrate competence on each of the skills based on the CAP from the standardized assessment.

9.5 *Motivation:* Given all of the consequences of prosocial and verbally aggressive interactions with peers, the student will identify all of the consequences for prosocial interactions with peers as those he or she likes and all of the consequences for verbally aggressive interactions with peers as those he or she dislikes.

9.6 *Beliefs:* Given a beliefs assessment, the student will identify all beliefs compatible with prosocial peer interactions as true and all beliefs incompatible with prosocial peer interactions as false. He or she will do this on at least two consecutive administrations with a 24-hour latency between assessments.

10.0 *Target Behavior:* The student will interact with peers in a prosocial manner without any physical aggression (e.g., hitting, slapping, kicking).

10.1 *Expectation:* When asked how he or she is expected to behave when he or she is with one or more of his or her classmates at school, the student will answer correctly with little or no prompting within 10 seconds of being asked. To be correct, the student's response must convey the idea that he or she knows that he or she is expected to interact with peers without physical aggression.

10.2 *Awareness:* After monitoring the frequency (i.e., number of occurrences) of unprovoked physically aggressive behavior in the target student over a predetermined interval, the teacher will ask the student how many times he or she thinks he or she engaged in such behavior. When the teacher's data and the student's data are compared, there should be at least 80% agreement between the two sets of data on two out of three intervals.

10.3 *Self-Control:* When the teacher monitors the frequency of obvious signs of anger in the target student and a small sample of peers, some with and some without anger problems on three separate trials, the target student's data (median score of three trials) more closely resemble the data (median scores) of peers without anger signs. The same objective is to be met by the student for frequency of impulsivity.

10.4 *Competence:* Given a standardized social skills assessment with a focus on socially appropriate interactions with peers, the student will demonstrate competence on each of the skills based on the CAP from the standardized assessment.

10.5 *Motivation:* Given all of the consequences of prosocial and physically aggressive interactions with peers, the student will identify all of the consequences of prosocial interactions as those he or she likes and all of the consequences of physically aggressive interactions as those he or she dislikes.

10.6 *Beliefs:* Given a beliefs assessment, the student will identify all beliefs compatible with prosocial peer interactions as true and all beliefs incompatible with prosocial peer interactions as false. He or she will do this on at least two consecutive administrations with a 24-hour latency between assessments.

Alternative Assessments and Interventions

Alternative Assessments

A number of these assessments are not commercially available. Please refer to the citation to access.

1. Anger

Children's Inventory of Anger
Nelson, W. M., & Finch, A. J., Jr. (1978). *The Children's Inventory of Anger*. Unpublished manuscript. Cincinnati: Xavier University.

State-Trait Anger Expression Inventory (STAXI)
Spielberger, C. D. (1996). *State-Trait Anger Expression Inventory*. Odessa, FL: Psychological Assessment Resources.
A self-report (paper-and-pencil) measure of anger in adolescents and adults (ages 13–65). Consists of 44 Likert-type items suitable for group use. Administration time is approximately 10 minutes.

2. Anxiety

The Child Anxiety Scale (CAS)
Gillis, J. S. (1978). *The Child Anxiety Scale*. Champaign, IL: Institute for Personality and Ability Testing.
This pencil-and-paper measure assesses anxiety-based disturbances in children (ages 5–12). Administration time is approximately 15 minutes.

Revised Children's Manifest Anxiety Scale (RCMAS)
Reynolds, C. R., & Richmond, B. O. (1978). What I think and feel: A revised measure of children's manifest anxiety. *Journal of Abnormal Child Psychology, 6,* 271–280.
A 37-item self-report measure that evaluates a student's feelings of anxiety across a variety of dimensions (e.g.,

physiological, worry/oversensitivity, concentration/anxiety, Lie Scale 1 and 2). A reliable measure of general anxiety in students 6 through 19 years; takes 10–15 minutes to administer; test–retest and internal consistency reliability and construct, discriminant, and concurrent validity information provided. Available from Western Psychological Services.

School Anxiety Scale (SAS)
Phillips, B. N. (1978). *School stress and anxiety: Theory, research, and intervention*. New York: Human Sciences Press.

Social Anxiety Scale for Children–Revised
La Greca, A. M., & Stone, W. L. (1993). Social Anxiety Scale for Children–Revised: Factor structure and concurrent validity. *Journal of Clinical Child Psychology, 22,* 17–27.
A self-report measure designed to assess anxiety in social situations for elementary age (Grades 4–6) students; includes 22 statements regarding feelings of students in social situations; takes 5 minutes to complete; test–retest, internal consistency reliability and construct, discriminant, concurrent, and predictive validity information available; not copyrighted; contact Annette M. La Greca, Department of Psychology, PO Box 248185, University of Miami, Coral Gables, FL 33124.

The State-Trait Anxiety Inventory for Children
Spielberger, C. D., Edwards, C. D., Montuori, J., & Lushere, R. (1973). *Manual for the State-Trait Inventory for Children*. Palo Alto, CA: Consulting Psychologists Press.
A self-report measure consisting of two 20-item scales for children in Grades 4 through 8. Administration time is approximately 10 to 20 minutes. A sample set may be purchased from Mind Garden, Inc.

3. Depression

Beck Depression Inventory (BDI)
Beck, A. T., Ward, C., Mendelson, M., Mock, J., & Erbaugh, J. (1961). An inventory for measuring depression. *Archives of General Psychiatry, 4,* 53–63.
A 21-item self-report measure, most frequently used with adults, but also frequently used with adolescents; good test–retest reliability and internal consistency.

Child Behavior Checklist Depression Scale (CBCL-D)
Clarke, G. N., Lewinsohn, P. M., Hops, H., & Seeley, J. R. (1992). A self- and parent-report measure of adolescent depression: The Child Behavior Checklist Depression Scale. *Behavioral Assessment, 14,* 443–463.
Completed by parents and adolescents, with two separate forms, each consisting of 15 items; factors assessed include negative affect cognitions and somatic/lethargic; for students ages 13 through 17; completion time is 10 minutes; demonstrated test–retest, interrater, and internal consistency reliability and construct, discriminant, concurrent, and treatment-sensitive validity; not copyrighted; contact Gregory N. Clarke, Oregon Health Sciences University, Child Psychiatry Division, PO Box 331, 3181 S.W. Sam Jackson Park Road, Portland, OR 97201-3098.

Children's Depression Inventory (CDI)
Kovacs, M. (1983). *Children's Depression Inventory.* Unpublished manuscript. Pittsburgh: University of Pittsburgh School of Medicine-Western Psychiatric Institute.
Most widely cited self-report measure of childhood depression; 27 items; factors assessed include negative mood, interpersonal problems, ineffectiveness, anhedonia, negative self-esteem; takes 15 minutes to administer; for students ages 7 through 17; demonstrated test–retest and internal consistency reliability and construct, discriminant, concurrent, and treatment-sensitive validity. Available from Maria Kovacs, University of Pittsburgh School of Medicine-Western Psychiatric Institute.

Reynolds Adolescent Depression Scale (RADS)
Reynolds, W. M. (1987). *Reynolds Adolescent Depression Scale.* Odessa, FL: Psychological Assessment Resources.
A 30-item measure of generalized demoralization, despondency, and worry, somatic-vegetative, anhedonia, self-worth; test–retest and internal consistency reliability and construct, discriminant, and concurrent validity information provided; 20-minute completion time; for students ages 13 through 18 years; order from Psychological Assessment Resources, PO Box 998, Odessa, FL 33556-9901.

Reynolds Child Depression Scale (RCDS)
Reynolds, W. M. (1989). *Child Depression Scale.* Odessa, FL: Psychological Assessment Resources.
A 30-item pencil-and-paper measure of depression; for students ages 8 through 12 years; 20-minute completion time; assesses despondency-worry, generalized demoralization-despondency, somatic-vegetative, dysphoric mood, anhedonia; test–retest and internal consistency reliability and construct, discriminant, concurrent, and treatment-sensitive validity information provided; order from Psychological Assessment Resources, PO Box 998, Odessa, FL 33556-9901.

4. Impulsivity

Gordon Vigilance Task
Gordon, M. (1983). *The Gordon Diagnostic System.* DeWitt, NY: Gordon Systems.
A continuous-performance test designed to assess levels of inattention and impulsivity; correlates significantly with *Matching Familiar Figures Test* (Kagan, 1966; see next entry).

Matching Familiar Figures Test (MFFT)
Kagan, J. (1966). The generality and dynamics of cognitive tempo. *Journal of Abnormal Child Psychology, 71,* 17–24.
Measures extent to which child is reflective (slow and accurate) or impulsive (fast and inaccurate); 12 match-to-sample items.

Self-Control Rating Scale (SCRS)
Kendall, P. C., & Wilcox, L. (1979). Self-control in children: Development of a rating scale. *Journal of Consulting and Clinical Psychology, 47,* 1020–1029.
Completed by parents and teachers; 33 items, 13 of which inquire about child's impulsivity.

5. Locus of Control

Intellectual Achievement Responsibility Questionnaire (IAR)
Crandall, V. C., Katkovsky, W., & Crandall, V. J. (1965). Children's beliefs in their own control of reinforcement in intellectual-academic achievement situations. *Child Development, 36,* 91–109.

Locus of Control Scale
Nowicki, S., & Strickland, B. (1973). A locus of control scale for children. *Journal of Consulting and Clinical Psychology, 40,* 148–154.

Multidimensional Measure of Children's Perceptions of Control (MMCPC)

Connell, J. P. (1985). A new multidimensional measure of children's perceptions of control. *Child Development*, *56*, 1018–1041.

Measures children's understanding of the reasons for their success and failures across four dimensions: cognitive (academics), social (peer relationships), physical (sports), and general. Consists of 48 Likert-type items.

6. Self-Efficacy

Children's Self-Efficacy for Peer Interaction Scale (CSPIS)

Wheeler, V. A., & Ladd, G. W. (1982). Assessment of children's self-efficacy for social interaction with peers. *Developmental Psychology*, *18*, 795–805.

Self-Efficacy for Social Skills in Children

Ollendick, T. H., Oswald, I., & Crowe, H. P. (1986, November). *The development of the Self-Efficacy Scale for Social Skills in Children*. Paper presented at the annual meeting of the Association for the Advancement of Behavior Therapy, Houston.

7. Social Skills

Behavioral Assertiveness Test for Children (BAT-C)

Bornstein, M., Bellack, A. S., & Hersen, M. (1977). Social skills training for unassertive children: A multiple-baseline analysis. *Journal of Applied Behavior Analysis*, *10*, 183–195.

Standardized role play measure; comprised of nine interpersonal situations involving assertiveness.

Matson Evaluation of Social Skills with Youngsters (MESSY)

Heavily researched social skills checklist; initial sample included 744 subjects between 4 and 18 years in private and public schools in the Midwest; unpublished.

Social Skills Test for Children (SST-C)

Extensively researched standardized role play measure; sample included 104 subjects from second to sixth grades from laboratory schools in Louisiana; unpublished.

Teenage Inventory of Social Skills (TISS)

Inderbitzen, H. M., & Foster, S. L. (1992). The Teenage Inventory of Social Skills: Development, reliability, and validity. *Psychological Assessment*, *4*, 451–459.

Developed for assessing the social competence of adolescents in Grades 7 through 12; 40-item scale; identifies adolescents with peer-relationship problems and appropriate target behaviors for social skills training; contains self-report information; demonstrated construct, discriminant, and concurrent validity; test–retest and internal consistency reliability information provided; takes less than 15 minutes to complete; not copyrighted; contact Heidi M. Inderbitzen, Department of Psychology, 202 Burnett Hall, University of Nebraska, Lincoln, NE 68588-0308.

Interventions

1. Behavior Modification

Kaplan, J. S. (1995). *Beyond behavior modification: A cognitive–behavioral approach to behavior management in the school* (3rd ed.). Austin, TX: PRO-ED.

See Chapters 2 through 8 regarding the design, implementation, and evaluation of behavior modification programs for strengthening and weakening behaviors.

2. Cognitive Restructuring

Anderson, J. (1981). *Thinking, changing, rearranging: Improving self-esteem in young people*. Eugene, OR: Timberline Press.

A program in cognitive restructuring for use with students "from about 10 upward." Consists of a paperback book with reading and writing activities for student use.

Gerald, M., & Eyman, W. (1981). *Thinking straight and making sense*. New York: Institute for Rational Living.

A comprehensive program in cognitive restructuring for students above the fifth grade. Includes activities, exercises, stories, and information for students, all in a student workbook format. Notes for teachers are included in the workbook.

Kaplan, J. S. (1995). *Beyond behavior modification: A cognitive–behavioral approach to behavior management in the school* (3rd ed.). Austin, TX: PRO-ED.

See Chapter 11 (pp. 381–424) regarding the design and implementation of cognitive restructuring interventions and the construction and validation of belief assessments.

Knaus, W. (1974). *Rational emotive education: A manual for elementary school teachers*. New York: Institute for Rational Living.

This comprehensive program in cognitive restructuring uses the format of a teacher's manual, with descriptions of several student activities for working on specific types of irrational thinking (e.g., mistake making, catastrophizing, stereotyping).

Nichols, P. (1996). *Clear thinking—Clearing dark thought with new words and images: A program for teachers and counseling professionals*. Iowa City, IA: River Lights Publishers.
An engaging program in cognitive restructuring for adolescents and young adults. Focuses on typical irrational thinking common to this population.

Vernon, A. (1989). *Thinking, feeling, behaving: An emotional education curriculum for children*. Champaign, IL: Research Press.
Available for Grades 1 through 6. Contains 90 activitiy lessons that use cognitive restructuring to help students modify their faulty thinking.

Vernon, A. (1989). *Thinking, feeling, behaving: An emotional education curriculum for adolescents*. Champaign, IL: Research Press.
See preceding entry; similar program, geared for older students.

Zionts, P. (1996). *Teaching disturbed and disturbing students: An integrative approach* (3rd ed.). Austin, TX: PRO-ED.
Describes an integrative approach to teaching students with emotional or behavioral problems; includes a unit with chapters that focus on understanding and implementing Rational-Emotive Therapy (RET) for children and youth.

3. Curriculum-Based Assessment

Howell, K. W., Fox, S. L., & Morehead, M. K. (1993). *Curriculum-based evaluation: Teaching and decision making*. Pacific Grove, CA: Brooks/Cole Publishing.

4. Direct Instruction

Price, K. M., & Nelson, K. L. (1999). *Daily planning for today's classroom: A guide for writing lesson and activity plans*. Belmont, CA: Wadsworth.
See Chapter 7 (pp. 63–77) for a detailed description of the direct instruction procedure, including sample lesson plans.

5. Problem Solving

Camp, B. W., & Bash, M. A. (1981). *Think aloud: Increasing cognitive skill, a problem-solving program for children*. Champaign, IL: Research Press.
Combines training in verbal mediation, self-instruction, and problem solving for elementary students. Available as a small-group program, designed for use with 6- to 8-year-olds, and three classroom programs, for Grades 1–2, 3–4, and 5–6. Heavily researched and field-tested on hyperactive and aggressive students.

Elias, M. J., & Clabby, J. F. (1989). *Social decision-making skills: A curriculum guide for the elementary grades*. Rockville, MD: Aspen.
A well-researched program in problem solving for elementary-age students.

Kaplan, J. S. (1995). *Beyond behavior modification: A cognitive–behavioral approach to behavior management in the school* (3rd ed.). Austin, TX: PRO-ED.
See Chapter 12 (pp. 431–436) regarding the use of a five-step strategy for teaching problem-solving competencies to children and youth in school settings.

Shure, M. B. (1992). *ICPS: I can problem-solve*. Champaign, IL: Research Press.
Three separate programs for teaching problem-solving skills to students in preschool, kindergarten, and primary grades.

6. Self-Instructional Training

Kaplan, J. S. (1995). *Beyond behavior modification: A cognitive–behavioral approach to behavior management in the school* (3rd ed.). Austin, TX: PRO-ED.
See Chapter 12 (pp. 425–428) for information regarding the use of self-instructional training in the classroom.

7. Self-Management

Kaplan, J. S. (1995). *Beyond behavior modification: A cognitive–behavioral approach to behavior management in the school* (3rd ed.). Austin, TX: PRO-ED.
See Chapter 9 (pp. 341–361) regarding the design and implementation of self-management programs for children and youth.

Kaplan, J. S. (1996). *Kid Mod: Empowering children and youth through instruction in the use of reinforcement principles*. Austin, TX: PRO-ED.
Teaches the fundamental principles of positive reinforcement and extinction to students from upper elementary through middle school and encourages students to use these principles to modify their own behavior and the behavior of their peers, teachers, and family members. Combines a direct instruction and structured learning (role play) approach. Includes performance objectives and

criterion-referenced assessments for measuring student progress. Refer specifically to Unit 5 (pp. 105–122) regarding the use of positive reinforcement in self-management ("Grandma's Rule").

Workman, E. A., & Katz, A. M. (1995). *Teaching behavioral self-control to students* (2nd ed.). Austin, TX: PRO-ED.

Demonstrates how teachers, counselors, and parents can help children of all ages and ability levels to modify their own behavior. New applications to more serious disorders often encountered by mental health professionals.

8. Social Skills Training

Dygdon, J. A. (1997.) *The culture and lifestyle appropriate social skills intervention curriculum (CLASSIC): A program for socially valid social skills training* (2nd. ed.). Austin, TX: PRO-ED.

This group-based social skills training program provides a structure for enhancing the social skills repertoires of children and adolescents that is appropriate across cultural contexts. Offers a structure for training on such targets as modeling, role play practice, reinforcement, coaching, and the use of a social problem-solving system.

Goldstein, A. P. (1988). *The PREPARE curriculum.* Champaign, IL: Research Press.

A comprehensive social skills program in textbook form. It includes methods and samples of materials for training in problem solving, interpersonal (social) skills, anger control, moral reasoning, and stress management, among others. Also includes material on classroom management and transfer and maintenance. Designed for youth (i.e., adolescents and younger children) who are deficient in prosocial skills.

Goldstein, A. P., & Glick, B. (1997). *Aggression replacement training: A comprehensive intervention for aggressive youth* (2nd ed.). Champaign, IL: Research Press.

A textbook on aggression replacement training (ART), a comprehensive research-based program for juvenile offenders. It includes methods and samples of materials for behavioral (social skills), affective (anger management), and cognitive (moral education) components.

Goldstein, A. P., & McGinnis, E. (1997). *Skillstreaming the adolescent–Revised: New strategies and perspectives for teaching prosocial skills.* Champaign, IL: Research Press.

A comprehensive social skills curriculum for secondary-level students.

Hazel, J. S., Schumaker, J. B., Sherman, J., & Sheldon, J. (1982). *ASSET: A social skills program for adolescents.* Champaign, IL: Research Press.

This group-instruction program includes videotaped material providing models of appropriate and inappropriate social interaction skills, lesson plans, training procedures, and skill sheets. Covers skills such as giving and accepting negative feedback, resisting peer pressure, problem solving, negotiation, and so on.

Jackson, N. F., Jackson, D. A., & Monroe, C. (1983). *Getting along with others: Teaching social effectiveness to children.* Champaign, IL: Research Press.

For students of elementary and middle school age as well as individuals with mental retardation between the ages of 18 and 35. Comes with program guide and skills lessons and activities for the 17 core social skills taught.

Kaplan, J. S. (1995). *Beyond behavior modification: A cognitive–behavioral approach to behavior management in the school* (3rd ed.). Austin, TX: PRO-ED.

See Chapter 10 (pp. 363–380) for how to assess social skills, choose social skills programs, and design teacher-made social skills programs.

McGinnis, E., & Goldstein, A. P. (1990). *Skillstreaming in early childhood: Teaching prosocial skills to the preschool and kindergarten child.* Champaign, IL: Research Press.

Similar to other skillstreaming programs; focuses on younger children.

McGinnis, E., & Goldstein, A. P. (1997). *Skillstreaming the elementary school child–Revised: New strategies and perspectives for teaching prosocial skills.* Champaign, IL: Research Press.

A comprehensive social skills curriculum for elementary-age students. Covers 60 specific prosocial skills including asking for help, apologizing, and so on.

Waksman, S. A., & Waksman, D. D. (1997). *The Waksman social skills curriculum for adolescents: An assertive behavior program* (4th ed.). Austin, TX: PRO-ED.

Utilizes reproducible blackline masters to teach appropriate assertive behavior skills to adolescents with and without disabilities.

Walker, H. M., McConnell, S., Holmes, S., Todis, B., Walker, J., & Golden, N. (1983). *The Walker social skills curriculum: The ACCEPTS program.* Austin, TX: PRO-ED.

Designed for use with students in Grades 1 through 6. Uses a direct instruction approach. Comes with teaching scripts for 28 skills and behavior management procedures. Video available.

Walker, H. M., Todis, B., Holmes, D., & Horton, G. (1988). *Adolescent curriculum for communication and effective social skills (ACCESS)*. Austin, TX: PRO-ED. Similar to the ACCEPTS program but geared toward the middle and high school student. Covers skills in three basic areas: relating to peers, relating to adults, and relating to yourself.

9. Stress Management

Goldstein, A. P. (1988). *The PREPARE curriculum*. Champaign, IL: Research Press.
A comprehensive social skills program in textbook form. It includes methods and samples of materials for training in problem solving, interpersonal (social) skills, anger control, moral reasoning, and stress management, among others. Also includes material on classroom management and transfer and maintenance. Designed for youth (i.e., adolescents and younger children) who are deficient in prosocial skills.

Goldstein, A. P., & Glick, B. (1997). *Aggression replacement training: A comprehensive intervention for aggressive youth* (2nd ed.). Champaign, IL: Research Press.
A textbook on aggression replacement training (ART), a comprehensive research-based program for juvenile offenders. It includes methods and samples of materials for behavioral (social skills), affective (anger management), and cognitive (moral education) components.

Kaplan, J. S. (1995). *Beyond behavior modification: A cognitive–behavioral approach to behavior management in the school* (3rd ed.). Austin, TX: PRO-ED.
See Chapter 13 (pp. 449–471) for information regarding strategies for the management of anger, depression, and anxiety in children and youth. Includes specific guidelines for using stress inoculation training.

10. Verbal Mediation

Kaplan, J. S. (1995). *Beyond behavior modification: A cognitive–behavioral approach to behavior management in the school* (3rd ed.). Austin, TX: PRO-ED.
See Chapter 12 (pp. 428–430) for a discussion of the use of verbal mediation.

Workman, E. A., & Katz, A. M. (1995). *Teaching behavioral self-control to students* (2nd ed.). Austin, TX: PRO-ED.
Demonstrates how teachers, counselors, and parents can help children of all ages and ability levels to modify their own behavior. New applications to more serious disorders often encountered by mental health professionals.

Publisher Addresses

Aspen Publishing, Inc.
1600 Research Boulevard
Rockville, MD 20850

Brooks/Cole Publishing Company
511 Forest Lodge Rd.
Pacific Grove, CA 93950-5098

Institute for Personality and Ability Testing, Inc.
PO Box 1188
1801 Woodfield Drive
Champaign, IL 61824-1188
(217) 352-4739

Institute for Rational Emotive Therapy
(formerly Institute for Rational Living)
45 East 65th Sreet
New York, NY 10021-6593
(212) 535-0822

Mind Garden, Inc.
PO Box 60669
Palo Alto, CA 94306
(415) 424-8493

PRO-ED, Inc.
8700 Shoal Creek Boulevard
Austin, TX 78757-6897
(512) 451-3246; (800) 897-3202

Psychological Assessment Resources, Inc.
PO Box 998
Odessa, FL 33556
(800) 331-8378

Research Press
2612 Mattis Avenue
Champaign, IL 61820
(800) 519-2707

River Lights, Publishers
308 East Burlington Street, No. 108
Iowa City, IA 52240-5810
(319) 354-0076

Timberline Press
PO Box 70187
Eugene, OR 97401
(541) 345-1771

Western Psychological Services
12031 Wilshire Boulevard
Los Angeles, CA 90025-1251
(310) 478-2061

References

Alberto, P. A., & Troutman, A. C. (1995). *Applied behavior analysis for teachers* (4th ed.). Englewood Cliffs, NJ: Prentice-Hall.

Bandura, A. (1974). Behavior theory and the models of man. *American Psychologist, 29,* 859–869.

Bandura, A. (1977). Self-efficacy: Toward a unifying theory of behavioral change. *Psychological Review, 84,* 191–215.

Bandura, A. (1986). *Social foundations of thought and action: A social cognitive perspective.* Englewood Cliffs, NJ: Prentice-Hall.

Becker, W. C., & Engelmann, S. (1973). *Summary analyses of five-year data on achievement and teaching progress with 14,000 children in 20 projects.* (Tech. Rep. No. 73). Eugene: University of Oregon Follow-Through Project.

Breen, M. J., & Fiedler, C. R. (Eds.). (1996). *Behavioral approach to assessment of youth with emotional/behavioral disorders: A handbook for school-based practitioners.* Austin, TX: PRO-ED.

Fad, K. M., Patton, J. R., & Polloway, E. A. (1998). *Behavioral intervention planning: Completing a functional behavioral assessment and developing a behavioral intervention plan.* Austin, TX: PRO-ED.

Gagne, R. (1970). *The conditions of learning* (2nd ed.). San Francisco: Holt, Rinehart & Winston.

Grossman, H. (1990). *Instruction in a diverse society.* Mountain View, CA: Mayfield.

Howell, K. W., Fox, S. L., & Morehead, M. K. (1993). *Curriculum-based evaluation: Teaching and decision making* (2nd ed.). Pacific Grove, CA: Brooks/Cole.

Howell, K. W., & Kaplan, J. S. (1980). *Diagnosing basic skills: A handbook for deciding what to teach.* Columbus, OH: Merrill.

Howell, K. W., Kaplan, J. S., & O'Connell, C. Y. (1979). *Evaluating exceptional children: A task analytical approach.* Columbus, OH: Merrill.

Individuals with Disabilities Education Act Amendments of 1997, 20 U.S.C. § 1415 *et seq.*

Kaplan, J. S. (1995). *Beyond behavior modification: A cognitive-behavioral approach to behavior management in the school* (3rd ed.). Austin, TX: PRO-ED.

Maag, J. (1988). *Treatment of adolescent depression with stress inoculation.* Unpublished doctoral dissertation. Arizona State University, Tempe.

Malott, R. W., Whaley, D. L., & Malott, M. E. (1997). *Elementary principles of behavior* (3rd ed.). Upper Saddle River, NJ: Prentice-Hall.

Mathur, S. R., & Rutherford, R. B. (1996). Is social skills training effective for students with emotional or behavioral disorders? Research issues and needs. *Behavioral Disorders, 22*(1), 21–28.

Meichenbaum, D. (1977). *Cognitive behavior modification: An integrative approach.* New York: Plenum.

Meichenbaum, D. (1985). *Stress inoculation training.* New York: Pergamon.

Meichenbaum, D., & Goodman, J. (1971). Training impulsive children to talk to themselves: A means of developing self-control. *Journal of Abnormal Psychology, 77,* 115–126.

O'Neill, R., Horner, R., Albin, R., Storey, K., & Sprague, J. (1990). *Functional analysis of problem behavior: A practical assessment guide.* Pacific Grove, CA: Brooks/Cole.

Price, K. M., & Nelson, K. L. (1999). *Daily planning for today's classroom: A guide for writing lesson and activity plans.* Belmont, CA: Wadsworth.

Rotter, J. B. (1966). Generalized expectancies for internal versus external control of reinforcement. *Psychological Monographs, 80* (Whole No. 609).

Stephenson, W. (1980). Newton's fifth rule and Q methodology application to educational psychology. *American Psychologist, 35,* 882–889.

Sugai, G., & Colvin, G. (1989). *Environmental explanations of behavior: Conducting a functional analysis* (2nd ed.). Eugene, OR: Behavior Associates.

Workman, E. A., & Katz, A. M. (1995). *Teaching behavior self-control to students* (2nd ed.). Austin, TX: PRO-ED.